Challenge The Hand You Were Dealt

Challenge The Hand You Were Dealt

Mark Knoblauch PhD

Kiremma Press
Houston, TX

www.authorMK.com

ISBN: 978-1-7320674-3-1

For those who have been dealt a bad hand at some point in their life, and chose to challenge that hand

Table of Contents

Introduction

For most of us, life cruises along with minimal interruption – we go to school or work, we take care of our kids, and we enjoy a little bit of free time every now and then. We may even allow ourselves to fall into a routine of sorts, becoming almost robotic in how we approach and deal with the events in our life. At some point, however, a personal struggle eventually occurs that must be faced head-on. In the vast majority of cases the struggle is relatively minor and allows us to trudge on, perhaps shaken by the incident but at the same time stronger for having gone through it. As you may have heard, it's not always the struggle that reveals the true worth of an individual; rather, it is often how life continues after the crisis has passed that ends up defining someone. This ideal reflects the words of George A. Custer who once noted *"it's not how many times you get knocked down; it's how many times you get back up"*. Some of us may feel like we've been knocked down too hard or too many times. And a few of us may feel as though we don't have the strength or desire to get back up.

You've no doubt encountered some sort of struggle in your own life, or perhaps you are close to someone who has had an unfortunate turn of events. During these times, somewhere within the condolences and support offered, you may have even heard those words that attempt to justify the situation that you or that other individual may be in: *it's just the hand you were dealt.* We've all heard the phrase, and we all know what it represents – that life has effectively dealt you a bad poker hand, and you're supposed to accept your poker hand with the understanding that you have no control over what happens to you. In effect, you are expected to give in to the pressure, the disease, the divorce, or whatever situation in which you might be involved.

The figurative poker hand that you can be dealt comes in a variety of types. And based on an individual's perception of their dealt hand, those events that can be considered as having been dealt a 'bad' hand can be highly variable. One's dealt hand may be on a grand scale, such as if you are experiencing a bankruptcy, or it may be on a much smaller scale, as might occur if you receive a speeding ticket or get into an argument with a neighbor. There is no standard classification for what qualifies an event as being the product of the hand that you were dealt; therefore, everyone is left to their own particular interpretation of an event as well as how much effect that event will have. It is important to remember, though, that how you perceive your own situation is not important to anyone except yourself.

When the phrase *it's just the hand that you were dealt* is spoken, it is typically intended to generate some sort of explanation as to the cause of an individual's downward turn, particularly in those cases where the recipient of the bad news or unfortunate situation just doesn't seem to deserve what has happened to them. It's almost as if the phrase intends to suggest that some strange force outside of our own capabilities is the true source of the turmoil, and as such we should just accept what has happened. In other words, it was just *meant to be*. For many of us, that may be justification enough to avoid fighting the situation. For others though, their mindset may be to put up a challenge to what has happened and try to improve their situation. If you are this type of person, I suspect you will associate with much of what is written in this book.

Assuming that your personal situation can in fact be made equivalent to a poker hand, it's safe to say that you can be dealt a wide variety of hands. You might be one of the lucky few who were dealt a veritable royal flush, having been born into wealth and generally able to avoid any real adversity during your life. Or perhaps you were dealt a hand you wish you could swap out given your daily struggles that might result from family issues, consequences of your upbringing, your neighborhood, or perhaps an old mistake you made. Regardless of what *has* happened, you have to decide whether you are accepting of the hand you were dealt or if you are willing to try to improve your situation. If you are the type that accepts what has occurred and are willing to adjust your life to embrace the effects of your situation, this book is not for you. Rather, this book is for those that do not accept what they have been dealt – those that don't believe that some higher power is controlling their life, throwing random events in their way just to make their existence difficult. Rather, this book is for those who wish to improve themselves or their situation – by challenging the hand that they were dealt.

If this is you, that type that fails to accept your dealt hand, take a minute to grasp the entirety of what you are taking on. You refuse to accept that your situation is due to some outside control, over which you have no power. And you refuse to accept that your life is the result of fate and you must therefore back off from any attempt to change fate's path. To accomplish these things, you must make a commitment now – in the introduction section of this book – that you are willing to do your best to make a positive change for yourself. That positive change must fly in the face of your current situation, to the point that it borders on the edge of unlikeliness, perhaps seeming almost impossible.

Given that you are reading this book, my guess is that you aren't content with the hand you were dealt and you want to look to improve your situation. Congratulations, you have taken the first step in that you accept that you have the *opportunity* to improve your situation, and it is in your control. Therefore, develop and reinforce a mindset that you must look to constantly improve your situation. We will discuss many of the ways to improve yourself in this book. Once you have made the commitment to make a positive change in yourself, the next phase begins in which you move from making the *decision* to start to one in which you actual make positive changes in your life that will serve to improve your current situation. And that is what this book is designed to help you do.

It doesn't matter what your particular situation is, for if you *want* to improve upon your current situation, the effort will be well spent. Few of us can honestly say that we don't have room for improvement, but at the same time it should be understood that there is a difference between needing to improve one's situation and wanting to make little changes here and there. But even if you are one of those who are happy where you are at – in life, at home, at work, etc. – there is most likely room for improvement that can make your situation even better. For those of you on the opposite side of the spectrum who are *not* happy with where you're at, remember the commitment you made just a page ago – to challenge the hand you were dealt – and work to get into the mindset to prepare yourself mentally to take on the challenge.

No one's situation is going to be the same, as unfortunate events occur across a wide variety of environments. For example, your own unfortunate personal circumstances may be financial in nature such as if you experienced a job loss, bankruptcy, or have accumulating unpaid bills. Or, the unlucky hand you were dealt may be medical-related, such as might occur in response to an injury, illness, or birth defect. Maybe your circumstances are social – you are timid, awkward, or maybe you have an overly controlling personality, and those qualities have led to a divorce, or drove you to commit a criminal act that remains on your personal record. No matter the situation you are in, don't fall into the trap that you are stuck with this proverbial 'hand that you were dealt'. Don't accept that what has happened to you is just fate. Or that it's what life, God, or the universe intended for you and therefore you must accept the situation. To have such a belief implies that these entities are secretly in control of your life, and that they have silently led you on a path that blindly forced you into your current situation with the expectation that you must continue on in life under their control, blindly accepting all future events as well. Said another way, accepting that you were 'dealt' your current situation indicates that you are not in control and therefore must submit to the greater force that controls our life. And unfortunately for many of us, we do just that. We accept our circumstances and we adapt our life to meet the expectations associated with those circumstances. Those individuals, quite simply, have accepted the hand that they were dealt.

What about those of us that don't want to accept the hand that we were dealt? Those of us who feel that *we* are in control of our life and as such, feel that we have the power to improve our current situation. For those of you who want to take on what life deals you, this book is written for you, for I too am much like you. I am a firm believer that no entity has power over the events in my life, and I am largely in control at all times. In my mind, life happens, and I exist within it. My own life is the product of a set of sequential decisions – both good and bad – and I am responsible for the outcome of those decisions. So no matter what life deals me, if I feel that I can improve upon the associated circumstance, I set out a plan to challenge my dealt hand.

Rest assured, I too have had my share of bad situations and unfortunate events. But for those times when I do make unfortunate decisions or have unfortunate events that end up throwing a roadblock (e.g. injury, financial issue, etc.) in front of me, I immediately begin to brainstorm ways to overcome the new negative event. I refuse to accept that I am trapped in a situation where I must sit back and let that situation play out; rather, I actively seek ways out. For each hand I am dealt, I throw up an immediate challenge to that hand with the full intent of being successful at my challenge. Because I have had success with challenging my own dealt hands, the tactics I have used in those challenges – as well as what I have learned from others – are what I outline in this book.

My motivation for developing this book stemmed from my observations of so many people over the years who felt that they had been put in a bad situation and should just accept what they were dealt. It may have been a medical diagnosis, an auto accident, or a divorce, but their attitude came across as though they were in some way supposed to simply accept what happened to them and adjust their life to allow the associated events following their incident to become some new standard by which they must live. A few, however, chose to challenge the situation they were presented, electing to 'power through' their circumstances rather than accept them. The consistent outcome of those I know who elected to challenge their hand was not only a better situation for themselves, but also the revelation that they were a stronger and more confident individual in the end. And this is what I feel all people who experience a negative event should strive to do. But it is not without commitment and it is not without preparation, and that is the focus of this book.

To be clear, this book in no way aims to be spiritual in nature, nor will it ask you to reign in some underlying force that exists in the universe. It is not to tell you that you are a wonderful person and you deserve what's best for you. Rather, it is written to help you look inward at yourself and figure out what personal resources you have available to you that can serve to improve your situation. And how to go out and actually make "what's best for you" happen. Such things like performing self-assessments, establishing your value, or altering your own negative behaviors, to name a few. By taking inventory of what you have available in conjunction with determining what you can offer – and matching those characteristics with the individual or situation that can benefit the most – you can hopefully see new opportunities for yourself that you may not have known about initially. In doing so, you can then begin to recognize your ability and launch a successful challenge against the hand you were   dealt.

Chapter 1: Establish your value

When looking at establishing various options for challenging the hand you were dealt, your initial focus should be to perform a self-assessment of the assets and attributes you have available that can help you counter the current situation you find yourself in. Therefore, in this chapter we will look at determining the value you as an individual possess. Your value establishes what you have to offer another individual, and as your worth increases, your ability to advance or improve your situation should be expected to increase as well. By your own inherent ability to improve your situation through the identification of your value, you also increase the opportunity to present a legitimate challenge to the hand that you were dealt.

You are probably familiar with the word *value*. Your understanding of the word may stem from a 'personal relationship' standpoint in that you recognize how people appreciate and recognize you as an individual. For example, there's little doubt that your parents, or your spouse, or a close friend values you as a human being. While this particular interpretation of "value" is certainly important, it is not the type of value that we are going to look at for the purposes of this chapter. Rather, we are going to focus on a second aspect of value, specific to *the usefulness of something.* As stated earlier, one of the ways to challenge the hand you were dealt is to improve the current situation you are in. Establishing your value can contribute to improving your situation by helping you to recognize what you have to offer. You can then better recognize where your value is most applicable, allowing you to match up your value with the *need* for that value. Upon recognizing that someone has a need for what you can offer, you will find that your potential opportunities increase dramatically.

You have likely come across this second description of value when viewing it from a monetary aspect, like how almost every time you purchase an item you subconsciously evaluate that item's value. Depending on a few factors such as your budget or the item's cost, you might even experience an internal struggle with yourself while contemplating the purchase – do you *really* need the item, such that it is critical for your daily function? Or, do you just *want* the item, in that it may make you feel more confident or help your day flow more smoothly? Either way you side, the mental process you put yourself through in deciding whether to purchase the item is based upon your perception of that item's value to you.

Think of value through this example. Have you ever went to change batteries in a much-needed item (e.g. a remote control), only to realize that the battery cover was held down by a very tiny screw? Your rush to get new batteries in the remote was quickly tempered by your frustration and a rampant search for a screwdriver small enough to do the job. At that point in time – when you desperately needed a screwdriver – what would you have given to have someone hand you the appropriate screwdriver? Five minutes earlier you had no need for a screwdriver and would have paid absolutely nothing. Suddenly, to have one easily available you may be willing to pay $5 or even $10. In other words, a small screwdriver suddenly has tremendous value to you because there is a need for what the screwdriver can accomplish. That is effectively the same thing that you as an individual might possess to the right person. The key, as we will discuss, is to match your value up with the individual who can most benefit from what you have to offer.

Understand also that value is highly subjective. In other words, value is perceived in the eye of the beholder, such that some individuals find value in an item while others find no value at all. In the example of the screwdriver, you had no need for it just five minutes prior, and therefore it had no value. At that moment in time, you would have laughed off the thought of needing a tiny screwdriver. Moments later, once you realized that you couldn't change channels back and forth between football games due to the dead remote-control battery, you were suddenly willing to pay a price to utilize the value that the screwdriver held. Based on what the item could do for you, you instantly felt that it held a significant value that did not exist just moments before.

You as an individual are no different. Whether or not you know it, you hold value to someone for some reason. Remember, we're not talking about the first type of value we discussed above, that generic "remember your mom loves you" type of value. While that type of value is key to maintaining close relationships, it doesn't necessarily establish your personal worth to other individuals such as a potential employer. Rather, we are talking here about your personal attributes – your knowledge, your training, or maybe your experience – that all hold significant value to *someone, somewhere*. These value attributes you hold may be important to an employer, a person wanting to have their lawn mower repaired, or someone who needs to get a better grasp of their finances but cannot afford an accountant or financial advisor. Because of the value-based attributes that you possess, someone else recognizes particular value in you, and you thereby possess a skill, attribute, or perhaps an idea that they can benefit from. What you have to do is match your value up with someone who recognizes and needs that value. But first, to challenge the hand you were dealt, you have to find and establish your inherent value in order to improve your life.

To better separate the two types of value we have discussed, let's outline it another way. Your mom loves you no matter your education, your net worth, or your interest. Those attributes have little value to her because they don't influence how she feels about you as her child. But, should a potential job opportunity instantly felt that it held a significant value that did not exist just moments before.

You as an individual are no different. Whether or not you know it, you hold value to someone for some reason. Remember, we're not talking about the first type of value we discussed above, that generic "remember your mom loves you" type of value. While that type of value is key to maintaining close relationships, it doesn't necessarily establish your personal worth to other individuals such as a potential employer. Rather, we are talking here about your personal attributes – your knowledge, your training, or maybe your experience – that all hold significant value to *someone, somewhere.* These value attributes you hold may be important to an employer, a person wanting to have their lawn mower repaired, or someone who needs to get a better grasp of their finances but cannot afford an accountant or financial advisor. Because of the value-based attributes that you possess, someone else recognizes particular value in you, and you thereby possess a skill, attribute, or perhaps an idea that they can benefit from. What you have to do is match your value up with someone who recognizes and needs that value. But first, to challenge the hand you were dealt, you have to find and establish your inherent value in order to improve your life.

To better separate the two types of value we have discussed, let's outline it another way. Your mom loves you no matter your education, your net worth, or your interest. Those attributes have little value to her because they don't influence how she feels about you as her child. But, should a potential job opportunity

22

(e.g. a remote control), only to realize that the battery cover was held down by a very tiny screw? Your rush to get new batteries in the remote was quickly tempered by your frustration and a rampant search for a screwdriver small enough to do the job. At that point in time – when you desperately needed a screwdriver – what would you have given to have someone hand you the appropriate screwdriver? Five minutes earlier you had no need for a screwdriver and would have paid absolutely nothing. Suddenly, to have one easily available you may be willing to pay $5 or even $10. In other words, a small screwdriver suddenly has tremendous value to you because there is a need for what the screwdriver can accomplish. That is effectively the same thing that you as an individual might possess to the right person. The key, as we will discuss, is to match your value up with the individual who can most benefit from what you have to offer.

Understand also that value is highly subjective. In other words, value is perceived in the eye of the beholder, such that some individuals find value in an item while others find no value at all. In the example of the screwdriver, you had no need for it just five minutes prior, and therefore it had no value. At that moment in time, you would have laughed off the thought of needing a tiny screwdriver. Moments later, once you realized that you couldn't change channels back and forth between football games due to the dead remote-control battery, you were suddenly willing to pay a price to utilize the value that the screwdriver held. Based on what the item could do for you, you come open, your education has high value to the prospective employer. How good of a son or daughter you are, how kind you are in your mother's eyes, or how good of a parent you are has little value to the employer. Which of those two 'values' do you think will have a better chance of getting you out of your current situation – that value determined by your mother or the value important to the potential employer? Undoubtedly, if you are intending to challenge the hand you were dealt and improve your current situation, the value that you have in a potential employer's eyes takes precedent. And that is the type of value that you must be focusing on when it comes to challenging your hand.

Remember to think of value as a representation of your underlying attributes. You undoubtedly possess many, but in your current situation they may not be getting applied appropriately. Once you identify and outline these attributes, you will need to match them with the individual or situation that will most help you improve your circumstances. For example, if you have office management skills, to a commercial fisherman you as an individual may not have much value because you don't contribute anything in particular (e.g. skills) that the fisherman might need (remember, we are not talking about things like valuing you as a human, which is something we *all* need to do). Or, to an attorney, you may not have value in that you don't possess a legal degree or certification that their practice could personally benefit from. While these might seem to be a couple of odd examples, we could literally go through every type of personality, career, or individual you may come into contact with and illustrate your potential value to it or them. What establishes your value with certain individuals largely stems from what you can offer, such that the more you can offer, the more value you have to that particular individual. He or she might then be willing to pay you a higher salary if you have experience in their particular field such as construction, or if you have knowledge about home gardening. The purpose of this chapter, though, is not to find who you have value for but rather to help you recognize and/or improve your own value. Then, you can later seek to match your value with the individual that can best benefit from what you have to offer, in turn setting up the best chance to improve your current situation and presenting a solid challenge to the hand that you were dealt.

Why spend time determining your value? The simple answer is that you can use it to help you move forward from your current situation. For example, if you were dealt a hand that never allowed you the financial resources to go to college, the jobs you have held might have developed in you a strong manual-labor type work ethic. Or if you spent years working in a firm, you may have over time learned what qualities make a strong leader and can teach others how to develop those qualities. In establishing your value, you can challenge the hand you were dealt by determining what you have to offer others.

If, for example, you want to challenge your hand by getting a better paying job, establishing your value can allow you to focus on those type of jobs that might help you to establish your expertise that will assist you in moving up through the ranks in just a few years, in turn improving your situation by potentially allowing for a better life than you had previously. Or, you may have been injured and now have a loss of function. By taking an inventory of what skills or attributes you still have available that could potentially benefit others, you may find that despite your injury you would excel as a motivational speaker, or an expert witness, or a consultant on how to improve workplace safety. The options for how your value might benefit others could literally be endless. Rather than focusing and dwelling on what you were dealt, you have to take the time and make the effort to move forward from whatever happened. One clear way to do that is to establish your personal value.

Depending on your background, you may not feel like you have much value because of some unfortunate past event like a firing or prior criminal act, or some other poor choice you've made. And to be honest, you might be right – if you choose to remain stale and stay around those involved in your past life, or associated with your family, or if you stay in your same employer's network. You see, by continuing to associate with those familiar with the "old" you, it can be difficult to establish your value because you are constantly reminded of other, negative issues. Associating with past issues or events prevents you from breaking free of the hold that can be tied into those past events. Furthermore, if you burned a few bridges, you might not feel like you can contribute anything of positive value, particularly if those people associated with the bridges you burned are vocal about it. Therefore, one major step you must be willing to take is to break free of your old self in order to make a fresh start, establish your new value, and re-establish yourself as an individual.

We've spent a bit of time so far discussing what value is and why it has importance. So how does one go about determining their value? The process itself centers on a thorough and deep self-reflection. In other words, you have to look inside yourself and figure out what you can offer those individuals who are important to your improving your situation, whether that be a potential employer, a mentor, a group counselor, or whoever/whatever has influence on improving your current circumstances. Establishing the value that you can offer then becomes a primary component of your connection to these entities.

In establishing your own value, recognize that we all have basic values such as love, compassion, etc., that we can offer. Because everyone has those basic values, they are not particularly important – not because they don't have worth, but because *everyone* possesses their qualities. Just like if everyone had the ability to get milk from a cow, there would be no market for milk. But, because milk requires extensive equipment and a laborious process to get to store shelves, we are willing to pay someone else to harvest that milk. Subsequently, the milk farmer has value, and we as consumers are willing to pay him or her a fair market price for that value of providing fresh milk. Similarly, because everyone can offer love, compassion, etc., you aren't recognized for having that particular value.   Instead, you have to look for intricacies about your own life that can better improve someone else's.

In working to establish your value, think about events that have happened specifically to you or qualities that you possess. This is not a time to be modest or shy; rather, be bold and a bit broad in your self-assessment. Events and qualities that you might come up with could be educational, such as a particular skill you have like the ability to tune up a 1959 Edsel. Or they may be psychological in value such as you have the inherent ability to find a fair solution in almost any conflict. Or, your value may lie in some type of experience or personal talent. Perhaps you once struggled with depression, or experienced bankruptcy, or lived through a flood event. Maybe you have been told that you write extremely well. Are any of these aspects possessed by every other individual? Absolutely not! And to someone out there, your having knowledge of these or any other particular topics could be of great benefit to them. Therefore, to a particular individual or group of individuals, you have value.

Once you start to establish your value, begin to also look for ways to tie your attributes in with other favorable aspects. Perhaps you have that ability to solve conflicts *and* you also have the ability to write really well. Your value and your interest has been established, and it is clear what value you hold – you should write a book outlining your technique for solving conflict! To *someone* out there, such a book would likely help them have an easier time with their own life. By sharing what you know, you establish your value and you become valuable to another individual. Or perhaps you are a romantic at heart and also write business memos really well, yet you have always wanted to try to write a romance novel. With such clearly outlined interests, why would you not take the logical next step? With just a little brainstorming, that hand you were dealt can get a freshly delivered, an in-your-face challenge brought about by the fact that you are able to write your own romance novel.

The same thought process can apply to almost any value you establish. If you have gone through depression, or bankruptcy – and you are not in fact a good writer – you could perhaps use your expertise in the area to counsel others, or give informational talks on the subject. Don't limit yourself by thinking that others probably won't be interested in what you have to offer. In a world of well over 7 billion people, you would have a hard time convincing anyone that there aren't a vast number of individuals who have an interest in something that you can offer. The trick will be finding those that *need* what you can offer, whether it might be advice, a skill, instruction, guidance, or similar.

Realize too that no matter your age, it is never too late to begin to establish your value. I often think of those that 'find themselves' later in life as a group of individuals who didn't determine and effectively match their value as early as most others do. Most of us establish early on what we want to do in life, whether it's run a business, own a home, or play soccer. But these are goals, and are not the same as value. As we age, our experience builds, and often we find that this experience can be used to help others. Your own view of helping others may be on a voluntary basis, such as through coaching or tutoring, or it could exist with a formal purpose in mind, such as might occur through consulting or a new professional offer. Regardless of the path you take, never feel as though age can be a hindrance to finding your value. Rather, view age as a quality that *strengthens* your value in that it has given you more experience and more knowledge to better establish the value that you hold.

So what exactly do you do once you've established your value? Simple – you assess that value and determine where it will best fit. Why? Because what you will likely find is that as you begin to put your particular values to good use, you will see improvements in your own life. Despite the hand you were dealt, you will realize that you can take any experience gained from your current situation (e.g. bankruptcy, injury, etc.) and use it to help others. I have done this in my own life, having been diagnosed with a disease that has been called "the most debilitating disease suffered by anyone who survives an illness". Despite this prognosis almost 10 years ago, I have had more successes and motivational drive in my own life *after* my diagnosis than I ever did before (more on that in a later chapter). Instead of bowing to the hand I was dealt, I took the opportunity to challenge it head-on, and have achieved accomplishments I never expected to attempt before my diagnosis. It is this same success that I want to use to help you refuse to accept your current situation and instead pursue more and better opportunities no matter your circumstances.

In summary, assessing your value helps establish a sort of 'inventory' of those qualities and attributes you possess that may be important to others. By recognizing what you have to offer, you can use your inherent value to help improve your own situation, such as might occur through the opportunity for a new job. You can then match up your value with the individual or entity that could most benefit from what you have to offer, giving you a new opportunity to effectively challenge the hand that you were dealt.

Chapter 2 – Develop your interests

We spent the last chapter talking about how you should work to establish your value in order to improve your current situation, particularly if you are interested in improving your career options. The value you can offer as a potential employee or provider of a service is important in that it can give you a chance to move up in your career or perhaps start a new career, both of which will certainly work to improve your situation. Some of you, however, might be thinking that you aren't interested in a better job or recovering from a bankruptcy. Rather, you are in a comfortable place and you might be quite content with your life. It may be that you have recently retired, or that you are ready to move into a slower-paced lifestyle and aren't looking for better job opportunities as much as you are looking to be 'fulfilled'. In such cases, it may be that you are more interested in finding an interest that encompasses your passion rather than looking for ways to improve your employment situation. Therefore, rather than assessing your value, you should view these interests and/or passions as a way of improving yourself. Engaging in either option can allow you to become involved and may ultimately take you on a new path in life. Therefore, be sure to make every attempt to engage in any type of activity that you find worthwhile.

Because challenging the hand that you were dealt is all about improving yourself as an individual, engaging with your passions – including both those you are aware of as well as those that you have yet to discover – can play an important role in that process. For example, if you were once injured but have recently found that you are able to jog, you might find that you have a new passion for going out for easy runs. A love for jogging doesn't necessarily offer value to anyone, but it could easily turn into a hobby, especially if you weren't able to do it previously due to injury. Without question, engaging in running activity can certainly be viewed as a mechanism for improving yourself such as through better health, but if you are like me, there are certain days in which the weather, scenery, and ease of the run just simply make the activity *enjoyable*. Then, you end up seeking that feeling again, making the run itself as enjoyable as the associated benefits of running. Such favorable aspects associated with your interests are common with things like hobbies or other activities that allow you to engage yourself in some type of productive activity. And in the case of running, if participation in such activities after being injured or inactive improves your overall mindset and perhaps even your health, you are automatically challenging the hand you had been dealt.

Much like we discussed with value in the previous chapter, you will want to match your interest or passion with the best recipient of that passion. Say you were obese at one point but were able to start to get the weight off through a walking program that over time turned into slow running. Eventually you learn that you actually *enjoy* running and you want to explore new avenues by which to take advantage of this activity. Therefore you look into finding a running group to join. This quickly finds you not only feeding your running passion but also interacting with a new group of friends. You may even find that running is as fun as cycling, and soon you develop an interest in trying a triathlon. Had you accepted the hand you were dealt during your obese days and chosen to just accept that you were supposed to remain obese, you may have never learned of the opportunities out there that ultimately ended up creating a whole new life for yourself. In joining the running group and being successful at something for which you have a passion, you not only introduce yourself to a new group of friends, but you have gained experience in health and/or weight loss that may be of benefit to others trying to lose weight. This could potentially open up opportunities for you in consulting, mentoring, or even public speaking depending upon your desire as well as your own results.

If you don't feel that you have any particular interests at the moment, pay extra attention to people and activities around you. As you do, you'll undoubtedly find something that sparks your interest if you are willing. If you take the time to conduct a little bit of research on the subject, you may find that you have a potential interest in that activity. This might lead to a visit to a gym, or to a show, just to 'check out' the environment and casually see if the activity sparks any excitement. However, understand that your potential interests don't have to be a type of physical activity; rather, you might be interested in joining a political movement, helping out at an animal shelter, writing poetry, or volunteering your time at a school.

In evaluating each possibility, you have the opportunity to become involved, thereby utilizing your talents in a way that can benefit others while also potentially making you feel as though you have a sense of purpose. Personally, I didn't have any interest in all at writing – until I decided to write a book. Once I completed my first book, and looking back at how much fun the process was, I found myself diving into the science and business aspects of how to write books. I became so enthralled that I eventually gave up my evening television-watching time to dedicate myself instead to writing more books. Now, my mind is constantly brainstorming new book ideas and rehashing old ones. This is all despite the fact that I had no interest in writing books until I was 44 years old. You might find your own interests in learning a new musical instrument, collecting items, or perhaps even helping others in various ways.

The act of engaging in your interests, whether it be learning a new hobby or pursuing a particular passion can help improve your knowledge and therefore your expertise as well. In each case, the end result will be a better, more engaged 'you'. By engaging in your interests, not only can you find a sense of purpose but you can also improve your overall value through becoming more knowledgeable in a certain area that could serve to benefit others. And in many cases, your interest can serve a dual role by not only engaging you as an individual but also improving other aspects such as through better health or being an asset to your community. Regardless of the immediate effects, engaging in your interests can help improve your value and will certainly serve to challenge the hand you were dealt.

Chapter 3 – Educate yourself

In the first two chapters we discussed how to take an inventory of the qualities, personal attributes, and specific interests that you have as an individual. Those characteristics can then be used to improve your situation, such as we discussed in dealing with a potential employer or running group. In matching your interests or passions with the individual/entity that can most benefit, your value increases because, in the case of a potential employer, the hiring individual can recognize how your attributes can positively impact the employer's job position. In turn, you can reap the associated benefits through perhaps a higher wage, better job, or more fulfilling life. Now, we are going to focus on how to contribute to you value through improving your knowledge, specifically through advancement of your education. As you improve your knowledge, your value immediately increases. This can serve to have a significant effect on improving your situation as well as providing an excellent challenge to the hand you were dealt.

One of the most beneficial personal qualities that can help you challenge the hand you were dealt is to become well-educated in some particular area in which you have an interest. This education could come through something as formal as a college degree or obtaining a certificate of completion, or it could be the result of years of experience in a particular area, such as might occur through an apprenticeship. Whatever path you take, you should develop the mindset to constantly seek out ways to educate yourself in order to generate a valuable tool that will help to improve your current situation.

Realize that possessing some type of formal education holds significant value. In becoming educated, you bring a level of expertise (i.e. a particular skill set) that someone will likely be willing to pay you for. And the more specialized your education, the more you will likely get paid. For example, if you have a high school diploma or general equivalency diploma (GED), you possess the same formal education level as effectively all other 18 or 19 year olds in America. Because so many people hold that level of education, you should not expect a high salary or outstanding benefits for any job that requires just a high-school diploma. Even though such an education is typically a requirement at many entry-level jobs, and it represents that you possess a certain degree of formal education, it does not hold particularly high value given that so many people have achieved the high school education. But at the same time, many entry-level jobs establish the high-school diploma as the minimum education level, so a diploma can be used as a standard that makes you *eligible* for a job but does not necessarily improve your chances of getting that job. Therefore, it is important in terms of education to obtain at least a high school diploma. But understand also that improving upon your situation and challenging the hand you were dealt may require attaining an even more advanced level of education so as to reap the associated benefits from that additional education.

If, for example, you are working as a laborer but want to move to the front office after a year, your formal high school education likely won't get you far, and you may have a hard time convincing the higher-ups that you are qualified to run the administrative side of the business. Instead, they will likely be looking for a formal college-based degree in business or other related field (e.g. supply chain management), and without that minimal standard of at least a college degree you will have little chance of getting the administrative position. Furthermore, the business world itself typically looks for a business degree – or in some cases a Master's of Business Administration (MBA) degree – as the *minimum* qualification for hiring. So, if you are armed with only a high school diploma you will essentially have little to no chance for getting hired simply because all other applicants will have at least a college degree. In other words, those applicants with a college degree will automatically offer more value to the employer than you simply by virtue of possessing a college degree.

Certainly not all jobs require a college degree. In those cases, employers will often look at an individual's experience in order to establish value. If you have worked in fast food for years but want to move into construction, be prepared that the construction manager will probably not find much reason to hire you given that you have no documented experience in construction. Even in manual-labor jobs you are expected to bring some type of evident value. Without experience, the employer may not feel that you have any potential to contribute enough to warrant a salary, and may instead be seeing the hindrance of your needing additional training, learning the policies and processes, etc., as reason *not* to hire you. So until you effectively get educated and thereby improve your value, in the theoretical situation of moving from fast food into construction you would not be able to challenge the hand you were dealt as your lack of value for that particular employer could make it difficult to move out of your current work situation.

Why does education have value? Quite simply, it allows you as an individual to provide a particular service to a company, individual, etc. For example, in a financial-based setting, a college degree would likely ensure that you knew basic terminology like *dividend* or *thrift savings plan*. A college degree, achieved on your own time, allows you to arrive at an employer armed with a set of job skills already intact that makes you ready to begin providing a service. This in turn ensures that the employer does not have to spend time training you on basic financial aspects and can instead invest time in orienting you to the particular policies and procedures of the financial firm. In other words, an education can help reduce the 'learning curve' time once you start a new job and allows you to immediately contribute to the goal that your employer has set out. Depending on the work responsibilities and duties, it should be expected that a college degree can set you up to be successful at achieving the outlined requirements of the job.

Because your ability to provide a service to your employer sets you apart from others, it's generally accepted that the more education you attain, the more you stand out from your peers. In turn, the more valuable you will become. Perhaps most importantly for those of you challenging a dealt hand that relates to improving your income, employers are generally paying you for the service you provide to a company; therefore, the more service (or more specialized the service) that you can provide, the more you can demand as a salary.

Think back for a moment to the milk example and realize that if you provide the same basic level of service as many other applicants, you will in turn receive a basic salary. However, if you have a specialized education, or you obtained additional training that allows you to provide a service that other employees or applicants cannot, then your value further increases in the eyes of an employer or supervisor. For example, you may have developed a special diet that allows cows to produce more or better-quality milk. Such a diet might improve the revenue of the milk farmer, thereby increasing profits as a direct result of the development of your special diet. Because you possess a value that allows you to improve profits, you deserve a higher salary than the 'basic' worker who is responsible for, say, cleaning out the stalls. But, your value required additional years of school to learn nutrition or a similar specialization. But because of the service you provided to the milk farmer, you had value – and leverage – to command a higher salary, or better working schedule, all of which you could not have provided without the proper education.

When it comes to educating yourself, know that the process of obtaining the education may not be easy, but it is certainly valuable. As a college professor, I tell my students to think of their education as an investment in themselves, and I recommend that you do the same. As a student, intern, or apprentice, you have to put the effort, finances, and time into bettering yourself in order to reap the benefits that come with the added value you acquire. Know that eventually the time will come that your education ends and you will be able to begin to reap the benefits. Sticking it out until that point arrives can be difficult and at times frustrating, but in the end the payoff will be well worth the effort.

As we discussed, earlier, what is considered as 'education' can come in many forms. It may be through the obtaining of a certificate such as if you become certified in CPR. It may be in the form of attending a seminar, such as one on how to improve morale at work. It may be through spending time as an apprentice for a stock broker, or a plumber, in order to learn or improve on a new skill. Or, in what might be considered the most formal method, it can be through obtaining a new degree, whether that be at a trade school, junior college, undergraduate, or graduate level. Regardless of the path you choose, the attainment of additional education will in no way detract from your value as an individual, and will only serve to improve your worth through the attainment of additional skills.

Remember what I said earlier – that education should be seen as an investment. Certainly, furthering your education is not without cost. For example, if you choose to pursue a formal education there can be significant financial cost that can reach into several tens of thousands of dollars over time. Depending upon your choice of a private or public school, costs can accrue quickly, and you have to ensure that you can see the degree through until the end, particularly if you take loans out. On the one hand, if you use your personal savings to pay for your schooling and you don't finish, you are simply 'out' whatever amount of savings you put in. However, if you take loans out to pay for your education, even if you don't finish your degree you will have to repay the loans as well as any accrued interest. Having the additional debt without anything to show for it in terms of a degree, certificate, etc., will only serve to amplify the difficulties associated with the hand you were dealt. Only when you can use your accrued education and improve your value can you then challenge the hand you were dealt.

There will also be a cost of time as well. Studying for an exam, practicing your trade, or attending a seminar requires time. If you do not have the ability to commit the required amount of time, you will likely not be successful in the long-term, or at least will not reap the benefits that furthering your education can bring. Therefore, take an inventory of your level of commitment regarding being able to commit time, finances, and effort, and ensure that all of them will work to set you up to be successful in completing what you set out to finish.

If one of your concerns about pursuing a formal education relates to having to attend college, rest assured that you have some favorable options available. One of the newer trends that colleges have embraced is the offering of online degrees. These allow you to obtain your degree in the comfort of your own home, accessing courses via computer. Online degrees have opened up a wealth of new opportunities for people who don't have the time or availability to attend college in-person. Given their online nature, the courses can be accessed in the evenings, on weekends, or whenever it is convenient for the student. There are a few limitations to online education, however. This can include fewer degree options at most universities than what a traditional on-campus student would have available. Also, some employers have yet to embrace the online degree option, so you should be aware of how your online degree might be viewed in a particular field.

In addition, if you are looking into the online education option, be sure and research the quality of the degree and the university offering it. Given the ease and simplicity of online degrees, there are many companies out there that offer online degrees but do not have accreditation, meaning that the quality of their degree has not been validated by an independent assessment organization. As such, many employers will not recognize an online degree obtained from a non-accredited institution. Therefore, if an online degree might be an option for you, ensure that you validate whether the degree you might be pursuing is offered by an officially recognized institution.

Although we have mostly discussed formal university-based education in this chapter, understand that challenging the hand you were dealt is strengthened by any type of education that you can give yourself. As we discussed, this includes not only the formal 'college-based' style but may include a certification program, a weekend seminar, or even an apprenticeship. Education is directly related to your value in that as your education increases, so too does your overall value. Furthermore, the more that you can specialize your education and make it unique from what others also learn, the more value you hold to any potential employer. This can in turn result in an improved opportunity for job advancement as well as salary. As you continue to improve your situation throughout your life, the foundation you set via your education can have a major impact in your success. Therefore, ensure that you have done or are doing what is necessary to give yourself the best opportunity to improve your education in order to successfully challenge the hand that you were dealt.

Chapter 4 – My story

We've been discussing so far the core aspects of what can give you the best opportunity to challenge the hand you were dealt – establishing your value, developing your interests, and educating yourself. In the upcoming chapters, we will outline a few ancillary aspects that can contribute to helping you successfully challenge your hand. But first, I think at this point it would be relevant to outline for you the process by which I developed this mindset that we have talked about in this book, particularly the mentality that forms the premise for why I feel so strongly about challenging the hand you were dealt. Therefore, let's take a detour from how to set yourself up to challenge your own hand and allow me to describe a bit of my own background. By doing so, you can better understand the premise for many of the ideals that form the basis behind challenging the hand you were dealt. Believe me, I have challenged my own hand many, many times. And in doing so I have been able to recognize that most all of my decisions are in some small way challenging the continual hands that I keep getting dealt, whether it be on a macro-level such as might occur in terms of hating a job (which I currently don't!), or on a micro-level as if one of my kids were sick.

In describing how I consider myself to have many dealt hands every day, I should also point out that your own dealt hand is based on perception – how you feel about your situation determines whether it is worthy of or needs to be challenged. Some may feel that their current situation is no big deal and they'll ride it out. Others may feel that they must put up instant resistance and deliver the strongest challenge that they can muster, as soon as they can muster it. Either way, deal with each challenge that you face as you personally see fit. Remember that how you deal with each is up to you, as you possess the ability to decide which events need to be challenged and which aren't worth a bit of your time.

As for me, I was born into a family of blue-collar parents who both finished their formal education after high school. I was an average kid – introverted, quiet, and always preferring to go solo rather than engage with others. My head was (and still is) disproportionally large for my body. I was never part of the 'cool' crowd at school (though now I look back at my friends from back in my youth and realize that they have accomplished so much more than the 'cool' kids have). And, I had a last name that made me an easy target for being picked on. Consequently, I was bullied quite a bit at a young age. More than most? Probably not. But, life was certainly not a cakewalk for me any more than it would be for others in a similar situation. From several viewpoints, I certainly didn't get the best hands dealt to me in my youth.

Growing up with my two siblings in a small Kansas town (population 3,200) in the high-interest-rate and punk-rock society of the 1980s, I have no issue saying that as a family were not well-off. We did not have what we wanted, but we always had what we needed. During shopping trips, I don't know if I ever had a successful request for a toy, or nicer sports equipment, and was instead always told to wait until my birthday or Christmas to see if it might arrive. My clothes were hand-me-downs, and most always two or three styles behind the latest trend. More than once I had to make my single pair of shoes last the entire school year, meaning that PE or recess was a matter of 'surviving' given that towards the end of the school year my shoes were at some level of falling apart. Jeans that started out dark blue were faded to an almost white color and had at least one leg marked with a patch sewn on by my mom. It wasn't what I would call hard times, but I equally wouldn't consider my adolescent family life as easy living.

Despite having what I needed, I saw the effort that my parents had to put in while armed only with their high school education. Even in my formative years I became aware of the struggles that my parents had in terms of finances. I saw the long hours of manual labor, heard the conversations about money, and became aware of what we didn't have compared to what my friends and their families had. I remember even back then thinking that I didn't want to always be the one that had to struggle financially throughout life.

And over time I began to realize that life in a small town like mine was severely limited when it came to income and job opportunities. Therefore, without much growth opportunity on the horizon in my small town I knew that I didn't want to remain trapped living there, bouncing from one minimum-wage job to the next in response to whichever mom-and-pop store closed down that week. Instead, I wanted the life I observed on television, one that allowed me to buy what I needed when I needed it, and maybe a few things that I wanted, when I wanted them. In fact, television helped open my eyes to what was 'out there' in terms of opportunity, and how I didn't have the same opportunities available in a small farm town. In hindsight I recognize that my childhood provided certain amenities like safety and security, close friendships, and low-cost living, but at the same time it also pigeonholed residents into that lifestyle. Instead of conforming, I felt at an early age that I had more to accomplish and instead chose to throw up my first challenge to the hand I had been dealt and move out of my hometown.

I established early on in life that I would be going to college. This was certainly not the expected outcome for many in my small town, with quite a few of my peers electing to stay on their farms or find work in one of the few businesses in town. Personally, I never had the mental fortitude or desire to excel at academics; rather, I just did what was needed. I graduated high school with a 3.19 grade point average – just enough to garner a couple of small scholarships but by no means enough to get my college paid for.

While many of my fellow graduates chose to stay in town and work blue-collar jobs – and were quite content at doing so – that lifestyle just wasn't for me. I wanted bigger and better things, including getting away from the small-town life – particularly the small-town mindset.

My first route was through a junior college, surviving on a books-and-tuition scholarship that was handed out in exchange for my throwing a javelin around the track. Around this time I found my career passion calling, and had to decide between continuing a track career and possibly earning some scholarship money or jumping full-on into my newly-discovered major. The only issue is that I couldn't do both. With track, the hours would conflict too much with my major, as I would have to complete an internship each semester of 20-30 hours. This same internship conflicted with my ability to work even part-time, so I had to make the choice of stopping college after a two-year degree – knowing I would not make as much money in the future – or continuing on with college through the accumulation of student loans. Given that my parents were in no situation to provide my tuition and housing, I chose the latter. I knew later on that the loan repayment would result in another bill, but I felt that the very fact that I would have a significant bill in the future, even if I quit school, would motivate me to continue. I had to do what I could to keep from having to move back to my small town, and I needed all the motivation I could get.

Because my career choice required passing of a national certification to enter the profession, I could have stopped after my undergraduate degree was finished. Doing so would have allowed me to earn a decent paycheck but would have meant I was relegated to many years of an entry-level position, one which allows you to do the minimum but doesn't put you at a level that has much success for career growth. Therefore, I had to weigh the opportunity to make a regular but minimal salary immediately versus investing more time, effort, and lack of income towards graduate school and the type of degree that was required in order for me to get the job I wanted. This is when I first recognized how education is an *investment* as we discussed in the previous chapter. I had to force myself to look at the long-term benefits as opposed to the short-term rewards. In leaning towards continuing my education further than what was required, I was also ensuring that I would be able to separate myself from other job applicants in the future as well as provide myself a better opportunity to get a particular job if I applied. But most importantly, I was keenly aware that I was challenging fate, given that I was 'supposed' to be back in my small town working at the local department store. I had to continue to establish my challenge to that hand I had been dealt early in life.

As I continued on with my career preparation I became aware of not only my formal education but also those informal, ancillary aspects of career building. Around this same time, I invested in building up my résumé as often as possible through volunteering, taking advantage of educational opportunities, and networking, all with the sole intent of helping myself to get into a good graduate program. This resulted in many early mornings as well as a few Saturdays in which I sacrificed studying to attend an event that I could include on my résumé. Remember, *everything* I was doing was with the intent of giving me the best opportunity to succeed. But, at a deeper level, I was proving that I had more in me than the life I had been born into.

Eventually I was offered a great graduate school opportunity – in large part due to the experience I outlined on my résumé – and soon afterwards I was deep into my Master's degree. With every homework assignment, presentation, and late-night studying, I was keenly aware of my goal of ensuring that I would not have to return to the small-town lifestyle of my youth. I maintained the mindset that to get the job I wanted, and to give myself the best chance at succeeding, I needed to excel as a candidate. So, being in an entirely new city for my Master's degree I had a wealth of new opportunities to increase my overall value to future employers. I continued my master plan – gaining additional certifications, networking, and learning new techniques. All in addition to going to graduate school and obtaining hours through an internship.

I had been motivated throughout my educational journey to be able to get my first job fresh out of school in a leadership position rather than spending a few years toiling as an assistant first. It all paid off for me as just prior to graduation with my Master's, I was offered my dream job. I had obtained a 'head' position fresh out of school while so many of my fellow graduates were accepting assistant positions. And even better, the opportunity was located back in a town 30 miles from my hometown. I could be close to home without the constraints of being in my small town. In my mind, I was set.

All went well for about the next year. Then, a run-in with my boss helped me realize that I could not continue to work for this individual. There was suddenly too much difference in our individual philosophies, and it all came out in one short meeting. Much of our tense discussion revolved around how to handle certain procedures, and given that I had been in my field for years while he recently came into the profession, I knew I was right but I also knew that he as my supervisor would not be budging. For a short bit I felt that I was trapped in my job and would be forced to concede to this new hand I had been dealt. I didn't feel that I had an 'easy out' given that I had just three months earlier bought a house. Though I was in a city, much bigger than my hometown, my job was the only one of its kind in town which prevented me from simply moving over to a new employer. No, to find a new job in my profession would require that I pack up and move – away from this previously-described 'dream job' that was just 30 miles from my hometown. It was a struggle to decide, as I could stay in my current job and remain a mix of miserable and fearful, I could stay in town and find a new job outside of my career area, or I could move to find a better position. Life had dealt me yet another hand, and it wasn't looking good.

So I did what I had to do to improve my situation – I immediately sent out job applications. I refused to let the job or the ties to my family being just 30 miles away force me to stay in an employment setting that I didn't want to be in. So, I took advantage of my years' worth of experience I had gained in my current job and sent out my applications for higher-ranking positions. With this experience and maybe even a few important connections pulling through for me, I was able to quickly land a new job, albeit 700 miles away. I had challenged the unfavorable had I had been dealt. Once again, I thought I was set.

For the next few years, I was happy. I was at a more prestigious and higher-ranking job with more responsibilities, making more money. But over time, the hours I was working (60+) per week in conjunction with the salary I was making ($50K) just wasn't going to be conducive for the long-term. I started to think of my options. I was reaching burnout. I didn't want to make a lateral move, even though some of those lateral moves could have made me more money. But yet I also realized that there were better jobs out there making more money for *less* hours, all in the same setting. And the more I came in contact with people who had those jobs, the more I wanted to be where they were. However, to get one of those jobs, I had to have a doctoral degree. But to get a doctoral degree at that time required full-time enrollment. With my schedule, I couldn't commit to that while also committing effectively to my current job. Slowly, I faced a new dealt hand – to stay in a job that had officially burned me out, or cut my ties, give up my salary and benefit, and return to the life of a full-time student. Again I had a house and had established myself in my profession and community. The question at hand was whether I was willing to give that up for the potential of an even better life/situation in the future. It was a decision that weighed on me for more than a year.

Eventually the burnout and lack of enthusiasm for my current job's outlook won out. I decided to throw up another challenge to my dealt hand. I quit my job and headed back to school full-time in my mid-30s. Now the issue at hand became making sure that my latest decision panned out. Soon I realized just how deep in I had gotten myself. I was enrolled in a very difficult PhD program, I was taking on new student loans, and I was having to try to make ends meet financially as I was now making approximately 75% less than I had been earning. During my six years of graduate school I would have to say that life dealt more hands to me than at any other point in my life. It was not easy. I was stressed. I wanted to quit *dozens* of times. But the drive for a better life as well as the realization that the only option for me if I were to quit was to go back to the same work setting I had just left was a tremendous motivator for keeping me on track. And six years later, after many emotional and personal trials, I emerged as a doctorate-holding graduate.

After it was all said and done, I find that I often look back on my time in graduate school and often wonder how I made it. No way would I ever do it again. The amount of coordinating, scraping by, and being the lowest of the low in the educational hierarchy took its toll on me to the point that I would never again subject myself to that. But now, I can comfortably sit here and look back on all of that with the satisfaction of being finished. Let me assure you, it's quite a different view when you look back on a major event as compared to when you are looking forward as the effort required *has been* spent rather than *will be* spent.

I had a vision for getting my doctoral degree as a means for challenging the hand I had been dealt, but I also knew that accomplishing that challenge would be a long road. In the end, I can look back and say it was a much longer road than I expected. And, I often realize that in the six years it took me, had I not made that initial step and quit my full-time job, I would still likely be in that same setting, knowing that had I made the jump six years earlier I would have been finished by then. That same mindset, of taking initiative early in order to finish early rather than later regretting not having started, has served me well in many situations. But in order to challenge that hand I was dealt at the time, I had to take the initial step. Having finally graduate, I could look back and be both proud as well as relieved at the success of my challenge. And all of the effort was validated by the fact that I ended up landing the exact type of job I returned to school for, and many years later I still enjoy going to work every day.

My purpose in telling you my story is not to simply outline my work history (even though I pretty much did just that). Rather, it's to help you understand the rationale for how I developed the ideal of challenging the hand that you were dealt. Had I accepted the hand that I had been dealt after graduating high school – one which had me destined for life in a small town – had I looked around in high school and thought that I was resigned to that setting, I would not have had any motivation to leave. I would be living in a century-old tiny bungalow, making $15 per hour, complaining that the price of gas went up $0.02, and probably excited about horseshoe or softball tournaments happening on the weekends. Not that there's anything wrong with that, mind you. But, I had bigger plans for myself, much bigger than the hand I had been dealt. A series of steps, taken at the right time have allowed me the opportunities I enjoy now.

Could I have taken a different path, making more money for less years of school? Perhaps, such as might have happened had I gone law school or some other professional program. But I didn't have the grades at the time, and I was happy where I was at for a while. But, given the free time I have now compared to the job before I returned to school, being able to spend as much time with my family as I do, with the salary I make, and the job satisfaction I enjoy, I am confident that my earlier investment to return to school paid off well. Even now, in this much more relaxed work environment, I provide value to an employer, and I bring unique aspects to my job that not all other applicants can provide. And, I appreciate the exchange I receive from the employer in terms of outstanding job perks and benefits. Looking back to the realizations I had made in my adolescence, I can say with confidence

that I was successful at challenging that first hand I
was   dealt.

Chapter 5 – Always seek improvement

As we mentioned briefly in the introduction, the phrase *it's just the hand you were dealt* is typically associated with a negative event in life. Rarely if ever does someone win a lottery or receive a job promotion and get told something along the lines of "wow! That's just the hand you were dealt!". Instead, the phrase is most often used after hearing bad news, or when someone is found in an unfortunate situation. Why this should be important to you is that even though the phrase is typically spoken in response to a negative set of events, there is almost certainly going to be some room for improvement. And given this room for improvement, it means you should be able to battle back from the divorce, or the medical situation, or whatever less-than-ideal circumstance you find yourself in.

Certainly, if you have been dealt a particularly bad poker hand in life, you should begin to immediately seek improvement. The improvement should occur not only in the specific area relative to the hand you were dealt but also in terms of your overall improvement. For example, if you recognize that a better education could help improve your situation, look into the options you have available for improving your education: trade school, certification, a bachelors or associate's degree, etc. But in order to improve yourself, you must first be able to recognize that there is room for improvement before you can begin to identify the areas for improvement.

When we talk about improving yourself, we are incorporating education along with *all* aspects of your life such as education, health, and financial matters. As such, no matter if you are looking to simply improve on your current situation or get yourself out of a bad situation, you should develop the mindset to *constantly* be on the lookout for ways to improve yourself. By improving yourself, you will in turn serve to improve your current situation – i.e. the hand you were dealt – as well. Many of the tactics that you can use to improve yourself will be discussed individually in this book, but we'll take a moment here to outline the *concept* of how to seek out the kinds of opportunities that can serve to benefit you as an individual.

No matter where you come from, no matter how far down in the dumps you've been previously, or how bad your current circumstances are, you have to think of your present situation as being at your worst. It doesn't matter how good or bad things are at the moment, just take the stance that you will not allow your situation to become any worse than it is at present. In other words, set out to ensure that right now is your *lowest* point. Even though things *could* be worse, or even if they have been worse at a previous point, you want to set your current situation as your new 'worst'. If things are going well now, work to ensure that they get no worse, and try to improve them even further. Set out to guarantee that from this point on, things will only get better as a result of both your attempts to improve yourself and through intelligent decision making. You took a vital first step already through buying a book that is designed to help you recognize how to improve yourself. Now you should also work to ensure that you both have the mental fortitude necessary to carry out your improvements and also commit to ensuring that you take steps to improve your life from here on out.

Depending on your personal situation, you might feel that you are at a low point right now, hovering around rock bottom, or perhaps existing in some degree of climbing your way back from rock bottom. No matter where you feel your situation exists, set "right now" as the new standard, a point from which you won't drop below. Establishing your new 'worst' allows you to make choices and engage in activities that only serve to improve your present situation. For example, if you are in debt, commit now that your debt won't worsen further. If you are in bad health, pledge to take action to prevent your health from regressing any further if at all possible. Recognize that any movement toward worsening your situation will only serve to subsequently worsen the effects of the hand you were dealt. And because that is precisely what you are trying to prevent, recognizing and taking action to prevent your current situation from worsening is of extreme importance.

The issue of not letting your current situation worsen any is not only relevant to 'right now' but should also focus on your future 'present' situation as well. In other words, try to forecast where your circumstances will be in two years, and ten years, and work to ensure that at each of those points also, your situation will be at its 'worst'. Even though in ten years your situation is expected to be better than it is now, you will want that point to set a new standard in terms of what your 'worst' will be. To state it another way, in ten years you should expect to look back on your current situation and think 'wow, I've come so far from where I was back then', but at the same time say 'despite my improvement, I will not regress from where I am now'. By thinking in this way and making long-term plans for your future, you help eliminate the possibility of regressing at all towards rock bottom, no matter what your hand initially dealt you.

Think about that again. *Every* decision you make, specific to those that affect your future as well as those (e.g. family) that can influence you – must be made with the assessment of whether it will positively improve you as an individual. Will buying a particular item put you into debt? If so, that new debt will eventually worsen your current situation. Will avoiding studying in order to go out with your friends affect your final grade? If so, you risk the consequences of a poor grade and the subsequent fallout (i.e. additional tuition, dropping out of college, etc.) from not passing a class. Will getting behind the wheel due to external circumstances (weather, inebriation, etc.) put you at risk for an accident or injury? A serious accident – particularly if combined with the influence of alcohol – will affect your finances, driving status, and potentially your freedom if jail time occurs as a result of your decision. You can't go back and 'undo' your bad decision(s). Therefore, you must try to forecast what *could* happen, and make the decision that leads to the best possible opportunity to improve as an individual.

Although these are just examples, if the decisions you 'want' to make in these types of situations lead you to results that will *not* improve you as an individual, you have to question why you would make the choice that you want to make. If you fall further into debt, or get a low or failing grade in a class, or get into an accident on a rain-covered road, how much more angst, debt, depression, or perhaps anger will you face when the consequences roll in. You might even get out of the situation without consequence (such as if your car rolls into a ditch but emerges undamaged), but will that lack of consequence give you confidence to try it again or will you recognize the luck you had and not press your luck further in the future? If you did in fact end up with an unfortunate consequence, there's no doubt you will look back to the decision you made and question yourself as to why you made the choice you did. In such cases, negative outcomes provide the unfortunate but clear answer to your original choice. The important thing for you to do is to determine if your actions will result in negative consequences that fail to improve either you as an individual or your circumstances, and instead make decisions that will serve to limit those negative consequences. In other words, making smart decisions will only serve to improve yourself.

Unless you are some kind of uniquely-strange individual, you know that making smart and logical decisions is the best course of action for improving yourself. There may be times in the process of making a smart decision that you are left with an empty feeling that leaves you to question whether you made the right decision, but that feeling is not likely regret as much as it is some unfulfilled desire left over from not taking the risky choice. If the choice you made – the logical choice – kept you from being any worse off than when you were initially presented with the decision, rest assured that it was the right choice. Remember, hindsight is 20/20 while foresight is nearly blind. Therefore, in those situations where I myself am tempted to make the risky choice, what helps me is to think of the negative outcomes that could result had I taken that risk. In each case, I assume that I would have had a negative outcome as a result of the less-logical choice. For example, every time I approach a stoplight that turns yellow, my first inclination is to rapidly accelerate through the intersection. My annoyance at sitting through the resulting red light is tempered by the belief that had I raced through the light I would have ended up getting into an accident due to some traffic event. Or, if I have the sudden urge to go gambling, the thought of spending an identical amount of cash on an item I truly need versus what I would spend at gambling is easily justified once I imagine losing that cash at a blackjack table. In my mind, I reinforce the logical decision in each case as having saved me from an automobile accident, or from effectively doubling the amount of cash I needed to spend (assuming I had lost at gambling and still needed to buy the item).

We've talked a bit about making smart decisions when it comes to improving yourself, but let's be clear – not all of us are put in situations that developed from our own choices. Those who suffer an injury or contract an illness come to mind. Even if we are in one of those cases, we still have to look to improve upon what we were dealt. If struck with a particular disease, we have to avoid the urge to withdraw into ourselves and instead seek out opportunities that allow us to flourish. You may not be able to do *all* of the things you want, but you must strive to look for ways that you can improve your own situation. Perhaps you could mentor others with the same condition, or write a self-help book about the condition, or engage in any number of other opportunities that are within your physical abilities. Remember, regardless of your situation you have value. As such, you have the challenge of triangulating that value with both your current abilities as well as with people who can best benefit from what you have to offer.

So far in this chapter we've talked about what it means to always look to improve yourself, but how exactly do you do that? As mentioned earlier, there are infinite ways to improve oneself – you just have to find the one that you would like to pursue. Therefore, the first step is to perform another self-analysis and determine what aspect you would like to make improvement upon. It may be that you want to learn better spending habits, or how to control your temper, or how to install plumbing. The next step is to simply take out a piece of paper and write down your interests or those particular areas that you want to address. Once you've done that, group each component into similar categories. This will allow you to determine what areas you should focus on, as those areas with the most items (e.g. learn how to manage money, avoid overspending, get better at saving money, etc.) likely hold most of your interest.

These interests you write down serve as the framework or foundation for how you are going to improve yourself as an individual. Once you have outlined your interests, address the underlying issue at hand. For example, does your list focus on health improvement, or money management? If so, look for ways that you can improve in those areas such as through attending a seminar or reading books on the topic. In doing so, you will not only improve yourself but you will be doing so in the area that best relates directly to your particular interest.

When we discuss the process of improving yourself, you must understand that improvement is not likely immediate; rather, it should be expected to be a lifelong process. You don't become proficient in a topic overnight, the same way that you can't just read a book and suddenly call yourself an expert on a topic (though some might argue that concept). Along those same lines, you might read *ten* books and feel quite confident about a subject, but let's be clear – reading alone does not make you an expert on most topics. Becoming an expert, which should be a goal for all of us when it comes to our personal interests, requires an educational process that involves reading as well as a practical (i.e. hands-on or field-based) experience.

The same thought process applies when it comes to improving yourself – strive to read as well as engage in related activities. For example, if you are wanting to lose weight you might feel comfortable going for a mile walk each night. To learn more about the *process* involved in losing weight, you could strive to read one chapter a day of a weight-loss book. While engaging in reading or practical experience alone is fine, combining both makes you not only smarter but also gains you a more well-rounded experience. That experience, such as perhaps counseling others about the barriers to weight loss that you experienced in your own health journey, or the initial aches and pains associated with dieting, or maybe even the ways you made time in your day to commit to exercise holds much more value to another individual in the same general condition who seeks your advice. In such a case, you have improved your value as a result of what you have learned, and you have also countered the hand you were dealt by failing to accept that you would simply remain in an unhealthy lifestyle.

Remember, improving yourself is not going to be a one-time act but rather a sum of many individual acts. In other words, engaging in something like reading a book isn't the only component involved in the grand scheme of improving yourself. Rather, it is just one part. As you later look back at the succession of these multiple individual components you'll realize that over time you have improved significantly as an individual. So, stay the course and maintain the mindset that improving yourself is a journey, not a single act.

Outlining my own experience with improving a little at a time might provide an example. For a while during my early years after finishing graduate school I wanted to improve my knowledge in my own area of study. To do this, I set a goal of reading one medical journal article per day on a topic in which I had an interest. Most journal articles tend to provide an overview of the topic as well as add a bit of new discovery; therefore, reading one article per day was highly beneficial at improving my knowledge in an area that was relevant to my area of expertise. But more importantly, over time I was able to look back at what I had learned over the course of a year, after which I had read over 365 individual articles that were all focused in a similar topic. It became clear that my overall knowledge in the topic area had increased tremendously. But to make this happen I had to ensure that I stuck to my plan of reading an article a day – even on holidays! While I was on one hand improving my knowledge daily in small amounts, after a full year I recognized that I had vastly improved my collective knowledge as a result of simply taking a small amount of time daily to engage in activity that was designed to improve myself.

This mindset has stuck with me even today. As the years passed my interests became quite varied, switching from work-based topics to areas such as training techniques for running a half-marathon, to running a marathon, to understanding educational standards, to tips on how to complete an Ironman triathlon. Each topic of interest that I settled in on called for a particular focus for a specific period of time (e.g. weeks, months), whether it be committing to a long run each day, which served to improve my health, or memorizing educational competencies and standards which helped improve my work performance – and thereby allow me to have improved job satisfaction and favorable annual performance reviews that help ensure some degree of job security. Each area of focus also has its own associated goal, such as completing a race or obtaining an academic accreditation. Regardless of the particular area of interest I was focusing on, I made it a daily goal of mine to improve myself incrementally. Over time, these small goals transformed into both vastly improving my knowledge as well as allowing for the completion of an overall goal.

Certainly in your own situation, journal articles and marathons aren't your only options for improving yourself. You might be interested in learning how to catch bigger catfish, for example. In that case, simple internet searches that provide results ranging from forums to dedicated websites about the topic can help to improve your knowledge. With so much information available to you at your fingertips via the internet, you can quickly become more knowledgeable about your topic, in turn improving your value. One caveat to internet-based information, however, is to remember that you must become adept at separating fact from fiction, as much of the material found on the internet is largely unregulated. As a result of this lack of regulation, almost anyone can post information regardless of its accuracy.

There are of course many other ways to improve yourself, and we will discuss in detail a few of these ways in the following chapter. For example, you can look into a formal educational course or seminar on a topic of interest, read a book, shadow a professional at their work site, or even take a class if one is offered. The end goal is always to be looking to improve yourself, which also serves to increase your value by making you more knowledgeable, perhaps in some cases allowing you to approach the level of becoming an expert. No matter if what you are aiming for is to simply learn a new hobby or if it's to enter a new career, improving yourself in some way is paramount to getting you on your way.

Although we have focused a lot on using education as a tool for self-improvement, realize that improving your mind is not the only option. For example, if you've been physically inactive for a long period of time, you may have a desire to get yourself into better physical condition. Maybe running a 5K is a goal, or a half-marathon, or a triathlon. Or lowering your blood pressure, or reducing your stress levels. Making physical improvements will certainly help prevent you from regressing any more toward rock bottom, and can usually be done with minimal financial investment. As they say, *a journey of a thousand miles begins with the first step,* and your own physical improvement is no different. I started my own fitness plan this way many years ago, making a daily goal of going one minute longer or 1/10th mile further than I had the previous day. After a few days or a few weeks of adhering to this goal I quickly realized how much progress I had made overall, which often amounted to a mile or two, or 30 minutes longer than when I initially started out. Favorable results are often the most effective motivation you can have to continue to improve, as you can see realistic results that validate the fact that your efforts have been successful.

No matter the improvement goal nor the mechanism you use to get there, it is essential that you have a mindset that you are constantly looking to improve yourself - both from the standpoint of your current situation as well as regarding you as an individual. As we discussed, constantly working to improve yourself helps ensure that your current situation is the worst it will be, and all future events will serve to improve your situation. Over time, the small incremental improvements you make will serve to contribute towards ensuring that you are constantly improving yourself. To challenge the hand you were dealt, you must be armed with the most effective arsenal, and in this case, that arsenal includes the ability to bring an improved 'you' to the fight.

Chapter 6 – Stay healthy

It goes without saying – if you don't take care of yourself, you won't be around to see how good your life might ultimately end up being. Your health is important, and it's one of the few things in life of which we can largely be in control. For many of us, we take our health for granted, often not paying much attention to our health until a friend has a serious event or until we are 'scared' into taking better care of ourselves after having our own minor health event such as a sharp pain in our chest, or maybe weakness in one of our arms. No matter the reason, maintaining good health is a key factor in challenging the hand you were dealt.

At first it might seem a bit odd to be discussing the topic of staying healthy in a book about challenging the hand you were dealt. After all, your health may be the very reason you are in the situation you are in, whether that be from an injury or a chronic condition. Nevertheless, our health is a major part of our daily life, and as such we need to ensure that we are giving ourselves the best chance to be successful.

A large part of ensuring that we have the best chance to challenge the hand we were dealt is through maintaining good health. When we maintain our health, we reduce the risk of having to spend extra attention on our health, allowing us to dedicate our time and effort to other areas, particularly those aspects that help us challenge the hand we were dealt.

We talked in the last chapter about establishing your current situation as the 'worst' that things will get. Even if your situation *has* been worse previously, remember that we discussed how you should develop a mindset that establishes what you are experiencing now as the standard for your new 'worst'. In other words, work to ensure that your situation becomes no worse that it is right now. If things are going well, keep it that way. If things are not going the way you want, work to improve them. And it goes without saying that your health is no different. If you are in poor health now, begin to look for ways to improve your health. If you are lucky enough to be healthy at present, continue to engage in activities that ensure you are able to *maintain* your health and possibly even improve it further. By doing so, you will help limit any potential influence that poor health can have on your current situation. In turn, you will be challenging the hand you were dealt by ensuring that poor health does not further complicate your matters.

Your health is not something that you should take on alone. If you are in poor health (or even if you are in good health), make the effort to find and work with a medical professional to get you on the path to better health. If you are over 40, get your annual

physical exam. If you have a lingering condition that you have tried to avoid seeking treatment for, seek out appropriate medical advice. These days, medical specialties are vast, and you should look to find the professional that best matches up with your current situation. In other words, if your health condition exists as the result of an injury or chronic condition, try to find a physician who specializes in that particular area. For example, if pain from an old back injury is limiting your activity, work with a back pain specialist who is knowledgeable in all treatment options – including surgery if you're open to it – so as to attempt to get you some relief and help you on the path to recovery. Furthermore, improving your health can have a few ancillary effects such as helping you become more confident, or more productive. And, improving your health also correlates with an improved quality of life as well as a longer life expectancy. In other words, healthy people tend to live longer. Therefore, any positive change you can make towards improving your health can help you live a longer – and hopefully more productive – life. Furthermore, if you are challenging the hand you were dealt, you are likely making significant improvement in other areas of your life as well. As such, improving your health with not only help you deal with those other issues, but may well keep you around longer to enjoy the benefits.

Therefore, even if the hand you were dealt is related to some non-health factor (e.g. divorce), improving your health or working to maintain your good health can help ensure you an extra boost toward improving the hand you were dealt. Events such as divorce can be extremely stressful. Similarly, certain medical conditions (e.g. hypertension) can be worsened with stress. Therefore, working to eliminate your high blood pressure can help ensure that it will not be aggravated in the event you have other highly stressful events to deal with such as a divorce. Even though no one *wants* to have stressful events occur, they will inevitably arise at some point. Ensuring that you don't have a concurrent medical condition to deal with can allow you to focus your energy on the stressful event rather than also focusing on the medical condition.

Think also of the financial benefits associated with staying healthy as you age. In the event that you are in poor health, you can expect an increase in medical visits, which will soon be followed by the associated bills. These medical costs factor into your overall expenses. Therefore, any improvement in your health over time that results in a reduction or elimination of those medical conditions that could affect you later in life will help improve your financial situation, in turn reducing your future debt burden that could arise as a result of having to obtain treatment for those medical conditions. This again outlines how maintaining your health can help you not only live longer, but can also play a role in limiting your financial expenses later in life.

For those of you affected by a serious medical condition that limits your physical abilities, in no way should you consider yourself limited by any means. In such cases, continue to challenge the hand you were dealt in terms of your particular medical condition by making sure that other health aspects do not worsen, particularly those factors such as excess weight, blood pressure, cholesterol levels, etc., that often increase in response to reduced physical activity or a poor diet. Failing to maintain healthy levels of these values is in effect giving in to your situation and accepting the hand you were dealt. This unfortunately can set you up for not only other related medical conditions but may make you more at risk for issues such as depression or loneliness as a result of your combined medical conditions.

When it comes to maintaining your own health, using the knowledge gained through medical research is one of the best ways to challenge the hand you were dealt. In this time of technological advances, you have to ensure that you take advantage of every opportunity out there. If financial limitations exist when it comes to your treatment options, an unfortunate but ever-present possibility, consider all options available to you such as government assistance, medical trials, discounted pharmaceuticals, etc. Remember though, that these are all considerations that you should be discussing with your personal medical professional, keeping in mind your ultimate goal of improving your health in order to help avert any potential medical issues that could distract from challenging that hand you were dealt.

Another consideration is to determine whether your health situation can be altered via your own actions. Obviously, intervention that occurs through a medical professional (e.g. prescription medication, surgery, etc.) is possible, but it's also possible that you have a medical condition that can be fixed through your own actions. In those cases, ask yourself if you are making progress toward fixing the issue that impacts you the most. For example, if you have high cholesterol, chronic fatigue, and high blood pressure in conjunction with being obese, have you tried losing weight in order to reduce the impact of the other medical conditions? Research is quite clear about how weight loss can improve cholesterol levels, etc., but if you are not taking positive action (after consulting with your medical professional) to reduce your weight, you are also somewhat accepting the hand you were dealt. Furthermore, the evidence is quite clear that these medical conditions don't spontaneously improve themselves. Therefore, if your health condition(s) is problematic now, or even approaching a problematic status, it will only get worse without positive intervention such as can occur through physical activity. If this is you, ask yourself if you are willing to live the remainder of your life in your current state, possibly regressing to an even worse state medically as time goes on. Hopefully you are not. But, challenging the hand you were dealt requires a bit of effort in the form of diet, exercise, and healthy life choices, all of which can be challenging.

I've been there myself. I myself remained injury-free until my mid-30s, never having even been inside of a hospital room other than to visit friends or family. I worked out, didn't smoke or take in any drug other than caffeine, participated in martial arts, and had extensive training in the medical and health field.

Yet, I was broadsided with the debilitating effects of my own medical condition that took several years to finally get a solid diagnosis. Severe vertigo bouts, constant unsteadiness, and random fluctuations of dizziness were just a part of my life. This led to depression, assured eventual suicide, and a general careless attitude toward life as a result of the situation I was in at the time. My mindset focused on establishing why I should care about anything else if I am in constantly reminded of or experiencing this incredibly frustrating, nauseating disease. You want to talk about lack of motivation? Think of being struck with one of the most debilitating diseases while you are still in in your mid-30s, expecting that you have another 50 years of life left to live with the disease. If you are like me, it's tough to maintain a positive perspective with such a grim outlook.

Having a medical condition called by researchers as one of the most debilitating diseases experience by people who survive any illness, I was subjected to random bouts of four to five hours of severe nausea, vertigo, and dizziness, along with constant unsteadiness. Once I received a diagnosis a couple of years after my first attack, I had the choice of living with this incurable disease, or taking the steps necessary to limit its effects. Obviously, most any individual would certainly begin the treatment immediately. Unfortunately, most treatments either don't work or come with severe consequences (e.g. no longer being able to drive) that I could not afford at the time. Eventually, I learned of a potential treatment requiring dietary modifications that had moderate success for a few sufferers. For me, quitting caffeine had significant effects initially, but once I cut my sodium intake to minimal amounts, I returned to almost 100% of my former self. Despite constant temptations for fast food, pizza, etc., the memories of the disease being at its worst keep me on track when it comes to sodium and caffeine intake.

While it would have been easy to simply accept my status and withdraw into myself once I received my actual diagnosis, I instead chose to dive into the research. I could have taken the low road, content to sit back and graciously accept what I had been dealt, but I felt I had too much left to do, and too many things left to try. The diagnosis became the new hand I was dealt, and I decided to challenge it head on. Initially, every time I tried to do one of those things prior to my diagnosis, I was slammed into the wall with a bout of vertigo, or left lying on the bed for five hours in a fit of overwhelming nausea mixed in with profuse sweating. It was as though I was helpless. But, the more I stuck to the recommended dietary modification, the more I was able to see positive change. My vertigo attacks stopped. The unsteadiness disappeared. Soon I realized that I felt almost 100% normal for the first time in over three years. This new diet quickly becomes a lifestyle for me, and for over six years I have had no instances of 'falling off the wagon'. As such, I have successfully challenged my own hand – one that had me constrained to a life of vertigo and nausea as well as the associated anxiety and need to withdraw from society – and am currently winning. And the return to normalness has been well worth the sacrifice of missing out on a few types of delicious foods.

When I was able to get back to what I considered 'normal', I made a commitment to stay healthy through adhering to the parameters of my dietary requirements. I went running more. I quit consuming excess sodium and caffeine cold-turkey. I was more diligent about what foods I ate. I started cooking all of our family's meals. And, I loved it all. A quick thought back to how far I had progressed since those earlier days when I was sick was all the reminder I needed to keep me on track, and for over six years I have yet to divert from my healthy living plan. And, I was driven by the fact that should be attacks ever come back, I wanted to know that I made the most of that period of time that I was 'normal'.

What I have accomplished in those six years could be simply described as 'miraculous' when compared against my days of stumbling, holding walls, or lying in bed sweating profusely and unable to move. I have now run several marathons, completed a couple of Ironman triathlons, gone hang gliding, and written several books. None of these events seemed possible when I was at my sickest. Had I sat back and accepted my fate of having this disease, I would be in no better shape than before it hit me. Moreover, I would certainly be dead of a gunshot wound. That is how bad Meniere's is, and such descriptions are consistent across those who suffer. But by fighting the hand I was dealt at the time of my diagnosis, I was able to find a successful way to suppress the effects of the disease and return to a relative state of normalcy. And

I have become a much better, more complete, and more driven individual as a result.

If you yourself are in good health, congratulations. You have a responsibility to yourself and those around you to maintain your health as long as you can. You certainly don't want to put yourself into a position where you are dealing with some other issue (financial, psychological, etc.) *and* you develop a health-related issue as well. Because some health conditions (e.g. ulcers, high blood pressure) can be generated from situations such as stress, etc., it is important that you do what you can to limit their occurrence. Besides, if you are dealing with one situation already, you certainly don't need to stack on an added health issue, particularly if those issues are preventable in nature.

To help maintain your health, be proactive in engaging in preventative activities. Eat healthy, engage in a physical activity program (after consulting with your medical professional), and engage in activities that can help limit your stress level. Many people often don't participate in much preventative activity until they or someone they know experiences a health-related scare. However, by then the situation may have progressed to the point that simple preventative activity will not be effective and they will instead need some type of medical intervention such as surgery or long-term medication use. This can then lead to significant cost along with the necessary time involved for rehabilitation or even picking up medications. All such activities serve to distract your time and energy away from anything you are already dealing with, in effect detracting you from spending time and effort dealing with the hand you were dealt. This in turn serves to possibly *worsen* the hand you were dealt. Therefore, if you are already in good health, invest in those resources which can help you maintain a healthy life and will in turn prevent your situation from becoming any more negative.

If you are not currently in good health, whether due to poor lifestyle choices or perhaps a genetic disease, you owe it to yourself and those dependent upon you (i.e. your family) to fight as hard as you can to improve your health. Having to focus on your health can add another level to an already difficult situation should you be dealing with some other significant issue (e.g. divorce, financial hardship, etc.), and it is important to try to limit the impact of your health-related condition so that you can better focus on any situations that factor into the hand that you were dealt. First and foremost, ensure that you are obtaining proper medical care whether that be through an initial visit to your physician or by taking your required medication. Failure to do so can and eventually will perpetuate your health condition, in turn giving you more to deal with and compounding whatever other situation(s) you are currently facing. Depending on your health condition, there may even be a reason to make your health the *primary* focus, thereby putting any other situations on hold. This is a conversation you must have with your medical provider as well as those close to you such as family, friends, and perhaps even your employer.

Whether you are currently healthy or dealing with a health-related condition, you must accept that maintaining your health is going to be a lifelong process. In fact, the older you are, the more involved you are going to have to be in order to stay healthy. Consequently, anything you can do at the present time to help prevent future health situations from worsening or perhaps from even arising is going to lessen the amount of overall issues you will have to deal with. As you have probably heard before, an ounce of prevention is worth a pound of cure, and this is certainly true when it comes to your health. If you are dealing with any other issue besides your health, by eliminating the opportunity for your health to become another distraction – or at minimum, preventing your health condition from getting any worse – will allow you to focus your resources on dealing with all of your other issues.

As we discussed, dealing with your health requires little investment. It may simply involve making better food choices that allow for a healthier diet. Or, engaging in 30 minutes of exercise per day. Over time, these activities are known to improve one's health, and you are certainly no different. You should use these lifestyle modifications as a tool to ensure that one major factor that you can control – your health – does not become a major issue that requires additional attention from you. Rather, your health can hopefully become an afterthought, existing in the background and performing at a high level in a way that allows you to deal with any other issues that result from the hand that life dealt you.

Chapter 7 – Stay positive

It seems so easy in this day and age to complain. We all do it at some point, and for many of us, we may even feel better afterwards. Unfortunately, negatively doesn't really serve to move us forward much. Rather, it can do a better job at suppressing our progress if we allow it to consume our thoughts and feelings. On the opposite side, maintaining an air of positivity can serve to help us see the good in everything, whether that's our work, another individual, or in this case, the hand that we were dealt. Given the vast associated benefits, there is little doubt that maintaining a positive attitude can be extremely beneficial for helping us improve our situation.

All of us love some degree of positive reinforcement – it's human nature. A 'congratulations' here or a 'great job' there can be just the motivation we need to press on and work towards our goal. While surrounding yourself with positivity is no doubt a benefit, it's equally important that we open ourselves up to being accepting of constructive criticism at times. Finding out that our plan isn't on track or that we are heading toward a pitfall or two can certainly be beneficial even if it isn't necessarily the news we'd prefer to hear.

When it comes to the hand we were dealt, many of us find ourselves in a bit of a compromising situation that doesn't exactly consist of rainbows and unicorns. Our situation may be the result of a debilitating medical condition, dire financial circumstances, or the loss of a loved one. In such cases it can be easy for us to regress emotionally, focusing on the negatives and allowing those negatives to effectively 'bring us down'. When challenging the hand you were dealt, however, it is important to avoid the negativity and instead accentuate the positives, no matter how sparse the positives may be in your particular situation.

Along the way of challenging your dealt hand, you will certainly hit a few bumps in the road. A plan will fall apart. A connection will be broken. Or a money-making opportunity will collapse in front of you. If this happens, it happens – you have to move on. Rather than lamenting in your misfortune, it is essential that you do your best to stay positive. Remember what we said in an earlier chapter – you have to ensure that you are at your lowest point and you should be working to avoid any potential regression to a worse situation than you are in currently. Otherwise, you might be tempted to withdraw back into the hand that you were dealt. Even though you may not be the type to see the good in everything, you should at least accept that bad things can – and will – happen. How you as an individual react to them is going to be key to your success.

One way I try to look at bad events is to see them as a learning opportunity. Thomas Edison once stated *"I didn't fail 1,000 times. The light bulb was an invention with 1,000 steps."* Hopefully we can all have such favorable optimism throughout our life, but even I myself don't have Edison's optimism. In my failures, I learn what didn't work. I made my attempt, but the approach I tried was the wrong one. So as stated earlier, we move on, strengthened by the knowledge gained in our failure while moving closer to the goal we are trying to accomplish.

When it comes to improving ourselves, we may have learned that our particular idea was not feasible, or that a friendship was not truly valid, or that we were not cut out for a particular event. Perhaps you learned that you cannot exercise on an empty stomach, or that a particular hobby requires better time management on your part, or that the expensive item you purchased didn't deliver the enjoyment you had hoped for. Despite the negative thoughts that may occur, remember also that in each case – in each small failure – you are strengthening your knowledge. And in strengthening your knowledge, you are also becoming more valuable to someone, somewhere. When these events occur, work to maintain an air of positivity when faced with difficult situations and recognize that there is a learning opportunity in there somewhere. Focus on how you learned that you need to remember to eat better prior to a run, or that you need to temper your impulsive spending urges. Even though you had a bad experience, realize that there is something positive to be gained from each, and that you have become more knowledgeable through your experience.

Remember also that the goal in challenging the hand you were dealt is to already have been at your worst. When that happens, it means that you will be getting better and better over time. Therefore, despite any negative perceptions, remember that you have been making improvement since your 'worst'. Any improvement should be viewed as an accomplishment on your part, and if you have achieved an accomplishment, that is certainly a positive aspect. Look at these improvements and find the positives such as how far you've come, or how you have achieved a milestone on the way to an overall goal. It's been said that positivity breeds positivity, so the more positive you can be, the more likely that you will stay positive. And having a positive mindset throughout your difficult situation can be one of the best things you can do to keep moving forward.

Another aspect of staying positive is that it helps maintain your open mind. If you are pessimistic, always finding or expecting the bad in every situation, you will be less likely to try new challenges. I am very familiar with this concept, as I was traditionally quite pessimistic. In fact, I was voted "most negative" in high school. This wasn't a ruse of any kind; rather, it helped me stay prepared for the worst by *expecting* the worst. And, I don't mind admitting that maintaining a pessimistic attitude served me well on many occasions. But over time, after having a few missteps of my own here and there, I learned that engaging in a positive mindset turned out to be much more productive and allowed the good to stand out from the bad for me in any situation. Whereas you are trying to improve yourself, you too should strive to stay positive in order that you can be more open to opportunities that are presented to you. Through maintaining a positive mindset you can provide the mental inspiration you need to continue on the path to productivity and success. This, without a doubt, is precisely the outcome you want when challenging the hand you were dealt.

Chapter 8 - Evaluate your behaviors

When it comes to improving your situation and challenging the hand you were dealt, you have to be willing to be humbled a bit as an individual. If you are not, you will fail at an important component involved in challenging the hand you were dealt. In this chapter we will hit on the aspect of being able to critically evaluate and refine your own behaviors. To do this, you will need to take an inventory of what particular behaviors you engage in and be able to evaluate whether those behaviors are helping you or hurting your ability to improve your situation and challenge the hand you were dealt.

Behaviors relate to the way in which a person conducts him- or herself. We all have behaviors, and each of our behaviors are individual and unique to us. You may think that being late is acceptable, while others see it as a major offense. You may have the mindset that as long as you can pay your bills, you are fiscally responsible while your friend may feel that he or she needs $5000 in the bank at all times to feel comfortable. They key to challenging the hand you were dealt is to evaluate which behaviors can detract from your ability to improve yourself and those which aid in your attempt. But one key thing to remember is that you *must* be honest with yourself in evaluating your behaviors.

Say, for example you are a procrastinator. Knowing that you've had undue stress as a deadline approaches and perhaps even had a few consequences of your procrastination, an honest assessment of this trait indicates that you will have to make a significant change in this behavior in order to challenge your hand. Even if you've been a procrastinator for years, you've found that putting things off tends to not only delay your having to still do the task but also ends up causing a backlog due to the additional activity that you have to handle. For example, if you put off mowing the yard until later in the evening, but it begins to rain in the late afternoon, you are consequently unable to mow for the rest of the day. As such, you will then have to mow the next day, during which you likely have other activities to accomplish. The next day, faced with the impending task of mowing that could have been taken care of had you tackled it the prior day, you now have to factor in an addition amount of time to mow the yard on top of everything else you need to accomplish. This can tend to cause you unnecessary stress as well as limit your remaining time available for getting things done. Had you simply mowed during more favorable conditions – i.e. when you had originally scheduled the task – your responsibility would be done and you could therefore address other issues with the time that you have available.

The same type of behavior assessment goes not only for factors linked to your personality but also for more easily recognizable activities, such as if you drink alcohol or use narcotic drugs. Drinking in moderation can be fine when it's done under the proper circumstances such as at home with friends or when you have someone around who can drive you home. But, if you instead take your drinking to excess, you can set yourself up for a whole new set of unfortunate circumstances that can include alcoholism or a DUI offense. Either situation certainly puts you in a much worse condition than what you are currently in, both mentally and financially as well as any potential criminal liability that you may ultimately face.

Remember too that no matter how you improve your behavior(s), you will want to ensure that you have incorporated the behavior improvement as a *lifestyle* modification. For example, if you are wanting to get out of debt, once you reach a debt-free state you cannot go back to your old spending habits or else at some point you'll end up in unexpected debt again. The same goes for improving your health. Once you reach a particular weight, or eliminate an illness, or whatever your goal was, you have to ensure that you are willing to continue on with the process that allowed you to reach that goal. Failure to continue or maintain the required process is almost a guarantee that you will revert back to the same old tactics that got you there in the first place. Therefore, make it a mindset that a lifestyle change is necessary to be able continue to challenge the hand that you were dealt.

As we stated, improving your behavior takes a bit of humility as well as honesty. You have to make an *honest* assessment of yourself, and be able to recognize which behaviors are truly a source of concern when it comes to being able to improve your situation. If, for example, you justify that despite having 37 pairs of shoes you still *need* the shoes you saw in the store despite the fact that you are trying to eliminate your debt, you might want to evaluate your spending habits. When you make an honest assessment of the situation, the reality of justifying the cost of the new shoes versus the fact that you already have several similar-looking pairs will probably help you to realize that it would be better to forego the new shoes and put that same amount of money towards paying off your debt. Or if, while preparing for your evening running activity to help you reduce your high cholesterol levels, you get a phone call asking if you want to come over and watch the game, the 'old' version of you might have said something along the lines of "I'll be right over". However, by performing an honest evaluation of your behaviors in which you realize that running will help you meet your goal as compared to heading straight to the game – and consuming some less than healthy snacks – will certainly detract from your cholesterol goal. Therefore, be on constant guard against the ever-present temptation, and be aware of what you must do in order to ensure that your behaviors help advance you toward your goal.

You may have heard that it takes 21 days to break a habit. I can assure you that breaking a behavior takes much longer. Many times, our behaviors are based around favorable things – such as watching television in the evening or shopping on weekends. But, these same behaviors may be what created the situation that you are in, such as if you went shopping at the drop of a hat and are now in a troublesome financial situation. My point in telling you this is that it can be difficult to break a behavior, as our behaviors make us who we are. This is in contrast to a habit, which can be often be less-than-favorable, particularly in those habits such as always drinking alcohol to excess, or being consistently late. In other words, expect that changing your behavior will take some time. In fact, a later chapter will talk about just that – how to avoid setting to short of timelines that ultimately end up causing you to fail at your goal. If you expect to change a negative behavior of yours overnight, you will almost certainly fail at that attempt. But, with a careful and well-planned strategy, you can evaluate your behaviors and help change those behaviors that do not advance you on the path toward challenging the hand you were dealt.

Chapter 9 – Use your time wisely

We have talked at length in this book about things you can do to challenge the hand you were dealt, and most of them outlined actions that you must take to improve your value as well as your situation. Now we're going to switch focus just a bit and look at a different aspect, one that requires you to organize your schedule in order to help eliminate wasted time. In eliminating time that you are not using effectively, you can in turn increase the amount of available, or "free" time that you have. By structuring your schedule you can help eliminate time crunches and also open yourself up to additional free time that you may not have had. This new time that you create can allow you to work on improving your value or engaging in your passions, or just simply relaxing in the additional free time that you have created.

It seems that we as humans are by nature procrastinators. We are given the fascinating ability to move and conduct work, but yet we are not inherently *motivated* to work. Instead, we find pleasure in relaxing, such as might occur when watching television or talking (or playing) on the phone. For many of us, our lack of motivation may have played a role in developing our current situation. Perhaps we were late to work too often, or passed up what we later found out was a good job opportunity, or maybe we decided to watch television rather than study. Regardless, a key aspect of challenging the hand you were dealt is to ensure that you are efficient in getting things done, particularly those tasks such as cleaning the kitchen or doing homework, so that you can focus more time and energy on those things that serve to improve your situation such as learning a new trade or participating in exercise. To do this, you will need to become adept at managing your time, becoming more efficient, and even learning to say "no" if necessary.

Challenging the hand you were dealt typically requires you to improve yourself in some way, either through learning a new skill or improving upon some facet of your life in which you find a deficiency. In either situation you effectively have to take on additional work/activity to improve yourself. Looking at your own life, do you have free time to commit towards additional activity? Most of us feel we don't have adequate time due to our involvement with family, work, and normal daily tasks. Therefore, we have to be able to take advantage of the time we have and become efficient at completing those tasks we already face. Doing so should help to free up additional time that we can then put forth toward our own improvement.

One of the first things you need to do when beginning to evaluate your efficiency is to look at how much time you have available in your day. Obviously, we all have 24 hours, and we all need to sleep. So, assuming 8 hours of sleep if you include the time it takes to fall asleep and the time it takes to effectively wake up, you are down to 16 hours. Assume 8 hours for work, plus an hour for travel to and from work, and you are down to seven hours of effective time. That is the time that you have to manipulate as necessary, but is also time normally filled with tasks such as eating, mowing the yard, running errands, etc. When it comes to maximizing the efficiency of how you schedule this remaining time, what can help you is to develop a structure that allows you to organize your tasks so that they are completed in the most efficient manner. This will then provide you the maximum amount of free time that you can use toward self-improvement, or even a bit of personal time if necessary.

I'll outline my own system, which over the years I have found success in overlapping individual tasks. The way that I do this is that I start with tasks that have some form of 'down time'. Doing laundry and running the dishwasher are examples of tasks that require some activity but then have a portion in which you effectively do nothing (such as once you start the clothes dryer). Once this down time begins, you might have an urge to go watch television or grab your phone to play games. Rather, look to immediately take on another task such as starting dinner, or cleaning a room, or some other activity that requires your full attention.

The intent in structuring your task completion is to get as much done as quickly and efficiently as possible, which will in turn allow you the maximum free time that you can then dedicate towards whichever activity you have chosen for challenging the hand you were dealt. What I have found is that if I invest my initial time at home completing as many tasks as possible, I will in turn have more time later on to complete whatever I *want* to complete. If this topic is interesting to you, I recommend that you read my book on how to improve your task efficiency, titled *"The Art of Efficiency"*, in which I explain in detail how task completion can become much more structured when organizing your tasks.

Another way to improve free time is to eliminate time-killers. As you sit down on the couch for an hour of television watching, ask yourself – do you *really* need to sit and watch that program? If it's educational in nature, I can understand the rationale for watching. But, if it's a comedy, or a reality TV show, what real benefit do you get out of watching? I ask this for a simple reason – it's precisely how I recognized my own time-wasting activity after watching a sitcom episode for what must have been the 40th time. Sitting there in my recliner, I remember asking myself how watching this episode again is going to improve me in any way. As I thought about it, I couldn't come up with an effective answer. So, I started pondering what I *should* be doing to improve myself.

I had already been working on a book, so I did some quick math in my head. Assuming I watched an hour of television with my wife per day, I could instead commit that hour to writing, and essentially have 30 additional hours of writing freed up per month. The following night, I started doing just that – turning off the television and turning on the computer. Since then, I've written seven books with a few more at some stage of completion. By recognizing my own time-wasting activity, I have been able to accomplish much more than if I had not recognized how much I was failing to accomplish by watching irrelevant television.

Take a hard look at your own activities in order to recognize your time-killers. If you play games on your phone for 30 minutes a day and also watch an hour of television, could you cut out 30 minutes of each and still allow yourself 30 minutes of television-watching along with 60 minutes of self-improvement? Remember, you're reading this book because you want to improve your current situation. If you simply can't give up your television show, that is acceptable, but is it worth being in the same situation you are in a year from now? If not, you have to go back to what we've talked about earlier – make the investment in yourself so that you will reap the benefits later. If you are watching purposeful television (e.g. educational or science-based shows) and don't want to give it up, consider waking up 15 minutes earlier and going to bed 15 minutes later, as that will give you an extra 30 minutes in your day. Just make sure those 30 minutes are *productive*. In other words, don't waste them! If you do choose to create time by getting up earlier and/or going to bed later, be cautious in depriving yourself of even this little bit of sleep. Doing so can have negative consequences during your day such as drowsiness that can negatively affect other areas. And if aspects such as job performance are negatively affected as a result of your reduced sleep time, you could end up worsening your current situation which would negate the entire purpose of what you are wanting to accomplish.

Much like evaluating your behaviors that we discussed in the previous chapter, being able to recognize your time-killers is a vital aspect for challenging the hand that you were dealt. The intent is not necessarily to cease your activity altogether; rather, the intent is to help you focus on those activities that help you challenge the hand you were dealt. This may occur through better structuring of your time as well as through eliminating those activities (e.g. television watching) that limit the amount of time and effort you can put forth to help improve your situation. Like many of the tactics we talk about in this book, finding and eliminating your time-wasting activity should be seen not as a sacrifice but instead as an investment, one that will help free up valuable time that can be used to help you reach your goals faster.

Chapter 10 – Plan ahead

The famous boxer Mike Tyson once said that *everyone has a plan until they get punched in the mouth*. This philosophy holds well for everyone no matter whether they are dealing with a personal or professional situation, because a sudden, unexpected event can throw off anyone's original intent. We go about our daily lives with the general expectation that events will occur without much interference, and this turns into almost a sort of 'expectation' given that it is our life and we feel that we are generally in control. Depending upon the hand you were dealt, you may feel the twinge of a bit of *lack* of control in your own life, whether that lack of control stems from some unfortunate prior event such as a DUI hanging over your head, an unplanned pregnancy, or some sort of medical issue that limits your capabilities. No matter the cause, it is essential that you develop a plan for how you are going to deal with each issue.

The problem with plans is that they inevitably take a turn for the worse. So often, what was supposed to be a succinct set of ten or so carefully scripted events makes it to around #2 or #3 before completely falling apart. Sometimes this is our fault due to poor or improper planning, while at other times it's due to events beyond our control. No matter the cause, it is important that we plan for inconsistencies in our lives so that we can take immediate *planned* actions. You read that right – when making plans, have a plan for when things don't go as planned.

There are two effective ways to go about planning for our plan to fall apart. The first is to carefully map out all of the viable possibilities that 'could' happen along with potential ways to avoid them. In other words, try to think of all the things that can go wrong and devise ways to avoid them from happening. For example, if part of challenging the hand you were dealt involves going back to school full time, one potential hurdle in accomplishing that goes relates to having available and recurring finances. Failure to make enough money to either pay tuition or pay those bills you will accrue can certainly have a negative influence on your educational plan. Therefore, recognize this possibility and try to think of ways to avert that particular outcome from occurring. For example, perhaps your class schedule will allow you to take on a full-time job, or maybe you can nail down some contract work at a frequency that will allow you to pay your bills. If worse comes to worst, could you qualify for students loans to get you through the difficult times. Or, it might be feasible to take out a student loan that you could use to live on, in turn freeing up more time to study or engage in other activity that can help improve your situation (e.g.

seminars, additional certifications, etc.). Even though loans will eventually need to be paid back with interest, if they can help improve your overall situation such as might occur through the receipt of an advanced degree, the investment may well be worth it.

The second way to plan ahead is to have a contingency plan in mind. Contingency plans are designed to be a backup for when things don't go as planned, and can help you avoid the problem of not being prepared for a particular occurrence. By having a contingency plan, or a "plan B", as soon as your original plan gets derailed, you immediately put your contingency plan into action. This help minimize lost time and allows you to continue on to your goal with minimal interruption. For example, if your plan is to get out of debt, and your first goal is to pay off your credit cards by December, do you have a contingency plan in place for when you suddenly realize that your car needs new tires? Perhaps your contingency plan would be to eliminate all fast food or restaurant meals starting October 1st, and instead using that money to contribute to your cost for new tires. Or, maybe your plan is to find a temporary part-time job that allows you to contribute more income towards your cost for tires. What should <u>not</u> occur is to simply push back the date of your debt-free goal, as that would tend to reinforce a mindset that you'll pay off the debt *eventually*, likely resulting in a few more extensions for your debt-free date. Having a valid contingency plan can help you stay on track, but your primary focus should be on creating a plan and taking the necessary steps that will help you adhere to the plan.

In addition to developing your plan, take the time to also lay out the endpoint of your plan specific to challenging the hand you were dealt. Start off by defining the goal you are pursuing. Even though you are challenging the hand you were dealt, at what point will you feel that you have succeeded? Without a clear established goal, you will not be able to measure your progress; therefore, you should have some sort of roadmap lined out that allows you to recognize the point(s) at which you have been successful. Evaluating these points over time can allow you to measure your progress as well as help you to recognize if you are *not* on track.

To illustrate the benefit of having a roadmap established to help you meet your goal, let's look again at a situation where being in significant debt is your dealt hand, and your challenge is to get out of debt. First of all, you must establish the point at which you consider yourself free of debt. Do you mean free of *all* debt, or just free of credit card debt? If your intent is to be free of all debt, does that include your mortgage, as well as student and car loans? Those larger type of expenses are generally considered as justifiable if you have a steady and sufficient income, and having them as debt does not imply that you are having difficulty managing your credit. But, it may take 20, 30, or more years to truly pay off all your debt, including that debt (e.g. mortgage) that even financial advisors feel is acceptable debt. However, if eliminating just the high-interest credit card debt is your goal, a more feasible and practical roadmap can be developed. If eventually successful, you would have succeeded in your challenge at that point that your credit card debt is eliminated, even though you might still have valid loan debts due to your home, vehicle, etc.

Without question, having a clear plan can be beneficial for presenting any challenge to the hand that you were dealt. Even though you may have a clear proposed timeline for accomplishing your goal, plans can quickly get derailed. When that happens, it is vital that you have effective contingency plans at the ready. Even the best planning can't prevent all mishaps, but when those mishaps do occur, an effective contingency plan can allow you to continue on your path with minimal interruption.

Chapter 11 - Avoid over-indulgence

To *allow oneself to enjoy the pleasures of.* With such a welcoming tone, the definition of 'indulge' actually sounds quite inviting. And how we as a society allow indulgence can occur in many different forms. We indulge ourselves in food, or fancy clothes, or alcohol, or some other aspect that brings us some degree of pleasure. When it's done in moderation, there is little to no harm resulting from our indulgences and we are free to carry on and reap the enjoyment the indulgence brings. If taken too far, however, indulgence turns to over-indulgence. When this happens, negative events often follow soon after. Over-indulgence in food can bring on excess weight and/or unhealthy blood values, and can end up requiring us to spend money on a new wardrobe to account for our subsequent increase in size. Excessive alcohol intake, as another example, can affect those close to us and possibly even put our lives in danger if we decide to get behind the wheel. In most all cases, the consequences of over-indulgence will eventually serve to worsen our situation. When that happens, it counters much of the effort we spend towards challenging the hand that we were dealt.

Finances are an easy way to analyze our over-indulgences. We've all been at a point where our finances are not where they want to be. We either spent too much money, or we failed to bring in enough money to make ends meet. If you experienced the latter, you probably spent some time looking for a better job, or explored ways to make additional money to help increase the income that you need. If you have ever had to go out and earn additional money in order to pay the bills, you quickly realized how much additional time and effort was required of you as well how it took you away from other important things such as family or perhaps even spending adequate time at your main job. But, bills have to get paid, so you do what you have to do. Failure to earn enough income will certainly have its own set of consequences, most of which (e.g. bankruptcy, debt collection, etc.) are much more severe in nature than what you experience in trying to earn enough money to pay the bills.

If you are on the other end of the spectrum and *spent* too much money, no doubt you experienced a bit of buyer's remorse in that you eventually regretted purchasing an item or wished you had not spent as much money as you did. This is not an uncommon occurrence by any means. While it's certainly nice to be able to buy nice things, it's even nicer when you can *afford* nice things. Knowing 'when to say when' is an important part of challenging your hand, especially if the situation that you are in is the direct result of over-indulgence.

Another way to state this is to realize that it's important to live within your means. Your 'means' can be anything from budget to diet, and represents your effective limitation that exists without causing you some kind of harm (financial, physical, etc.). For example, buying items you cannot afford puts you beyond your financial means and will almost certainly end up *worsening* the hand you were dealt. In a case such as this you will likely experience buyer's remorse – a type of regret that can mimic mild depression – which detracts from any progress you are making towards improving your overall situation. Furthermore, you will have to address the actual financial impact of the situation, particularly that aspect surrounding the fact that the money you spent could have been better used for paying your phone or electricity bill.

To understand overindulgence, we have to first outline what it means to *indulge.* Indulgence is the act of letting yourself enjoy something. If you love a certain television show, for example, you likely indulge in it every week that it comes on. Indulgence is not a problem as long as we stay within certain parameters, such as if the activity does not interfere with important responsibilities (e.g. cleaning, family time), we can afford it, and it is not detrimental to society or our health (e.g. drug use). The issue is when indulgence turns to *over-indulgence,* or the act of participating in something to excessive levels. For example, it is perfectly acceptable to go gambling if

113

you have money available. But, if you use money set aside for paying bills to gamble, you have went from indulgence to over-indulgence simply because of the original intent of the money. Assuming you lose at gambling, you will not only be out that particular amount of money, but you will also have to find a way to make that money back in order to pay the required bills. This then worsens your current situation through added work hours or required contract work, and can affect other aspects of life through induced stress, lack of sleep, regret, or possibly even anger.

Remember back to an earlier chapter where we discussed that in order to challenge the hand you were dealt, you have to be able to continue to work to ensure that your current situation is your worst situation. If unforeseen issues such as an illness arise, that is acceptable given that you were not the direct cause. However, if you induce your own issues as a result of over-indulgence, such as losing a significant amount of money gambling which you had already marked for other, more important uses, the additional conflict this will cause can be quite problematic and will certainly create a worse situation that you had been in, even if for only a short time.

Therefore, work to recognize the difference between indulgence and over-indulgence in your own life. Indulgence comes in many shapes, as does over-indulgence, and it takes a very aware mind to recognize the point at which a simple pleasure turns into an obsession or an addiction. Therefore, be aware of the risks that come with the decisions you make regarding diet, clothing, finances, etc., and always remember that making the logical choice will serve you best when it comes to challenging the hand you were dealt. For example, if finances are one of your issues, look to delay those purchases that you want but can't afford – such as a vacation or a motorcycle – until you have a valid way to pay the bill other than to simply put everything on credit. By using sound judgment in your decisions, you can ensure that there are no unexpected issues that arise on your path to challenging the hand you were dealt.

Chapter 12 – Take advantage of opportunities

Improving upon your current situation is not a passive task. In other words, you can't sit back and expect that your situation will just become better on its own. Even winning a lottery requires an individual to go out and buy a ticket. Improving yourself is similar, without quite as big of a payoff. And, improvement does not typically come with a single investment of time or effort. Rather, one should expect a series of small investments (e.g. time, effort, money, etc.) that over time can be rewarded with you ending up being in a better situation than when you started. To improve the hand you were dealt, you have to begin to look for – and take advantage of – opportunities that can serve to improve your current situation. Investing in these opportunities can in turn provide you an outstanding opportunity to challenge the hand that you were dealt.

As stated above, improvement is not a process that always occurs on its own. Rather, you have to both seek out and engage in activities and events that work to improve you as a person as well as your situation. When those opportunities occur, it is important that you are able to both recognize the opportunity as well as engage yourself to take the necessary action. In doing so, you will be able to be able to expose yourself to a significant opportunity for growth and improvement that will certainly benefit you on your journey.

One important thing to remember is to never pass up an opportunity to interact with other individuals. These interactions can occur in a very subtle setting, such as helping some friends move, or it can be more formal such as might occur if you were asked to give a professional talk. The reason it is important to engage in opportunities is because these can be a way for you to exposure yourself and your value to others, almost a type of free marketing (discussed in an upcoming chapter). You may not even have direct impact upon someone, but those individuals you are interacting with may interact with others, who know a friend who can benefit from your value. Eventually the word gets back to you, and you have at that point established a connection that can be turned into a favorable opportunity. Perhaps you can mentor someone, or learn a skill, or speak to a group of affected individuals about your own experience. In doing so, you then make new connections, which if you have made a good impression, can lead to future opportunities. And it all may have happened as the result of a discreet, even brief interaction you had with someone.

Through one simple discrete connection, you could initiate an entirely new path in life. This may lead to speaking engagements, or a new group of friends to hang out with, or perhaps even something like a book deal. But none of it would have been possible had you not made the initial connection, a connection which at the time you may have felt was inconspicuous and unremarkable. And that key point is why it is essential that you work to take advantage of opportunities that present themselves.

Simply put, the more opportunities you take advantage of, the more connections you make. Each person that you connect with has a group of friends, and that group may or may not have similar interests as what you are aiming to achieve. Each of those friends then has a group of additional friends as well. Just one connection, or better yet several connections at a single event, can jump start you on your way to challenging the hand you were dealt. If you are wanting to further your education, perhaps you meet someone in a relevant academic program. Or, you meet someone who can play an instrument that you want to learn. Or you interact with someone involved in mentoring a group of individuals with a similar condition. To give yourself the best chance of making these kinds of connections happen, you have to ensure that you take advantage of every opportunity presented.

Once you've made the connection, you have to take steps to follow through on the mutual interest. If the person is coming to you for assistance, mentoring, or your professional advice such as through a consulting opportunity, get their phone number and initiate the first call. If you are seeking advice or assistance, or if another individual can set you up with someone or something that can improve your situation, ensure that they have your phone number, and give them a reason to call.

Understand also that taking advantage of opportunities means that you will have to make a few sacrifices. A little bit of free time here or there may be interrupted by an opportunity to meet with others that can serve to improve yourself. You have to then weigh the risk/reward in order to make the determination of whether the proposed opportunity can benefit you as an individual (beyond the normal occurrence of simply helping someone out, which may not necessarily benefit you).

Know also that everyone has their limits. Even though taking advantage of an opportunity can benefit you, you should also be aware that there may be times that you just simply have to say "no". Don't let yourself get taken advantage of, and be clear with yourself about those times when you are too busy to take advantage of an opportunity. I myself have turned down plenty of opportunities simply because the trip was too far, or it would keep me away from a family event. Yet at the same time, the decisions to turn down opportunities often came in response to my recognizing that the opportunity was not a 'golden' opportunity, or one that held the potential to have a significant impact in my situation. Rather, events that I have turned down were what I considered a 'minor' opportunity, and for me the risk (e.g. traffic, time away from home, etc.) was not worth the reward (e.g. speaking to a few people). You should perform a similar type of assessment each time you encounter an opportunity that could work to improve your own situation.

Because you are looking to challenge the hand you were dealt, you have to be willing to step outside of your personal box and expand your opportunities. Meet people, help out at events, and engage yourself in ways that will serve to improve you as an individual. You can then use that improvement to your advantage in any number of ways, in turn building up the opportunity to challenge the hand you were dealt.

Chapter 13 – Improve your marketability

As we have discussed at length, challenging the hand that you were dealt revolves around improving your situation through one of several different ways. Now, we're going to take a detour in order to look at how you can help make others aware of what you have to offer, particularly in the value that you can offer. Remember how we stated in the first chapter that you need to match up your value with the individual who would most benefit? To do that you have to find a way to make him or her (e.g. an employer, a potential client, etc.) aware of what you have to offer. In other words, you need to be able to properly market yourself.

Marketing can be a very complex strategy if you allow it to become such. Think about it – whole college majors are dedicated to the science of getting the word out effectively, whether it be for a product, an idea, or a person. Therefore, be aware that if you recognize the potential you possess when backed by good marketing, there are a wealth of books out there that are very detailed on the topic of self-marketing and may be of great benefit to you. Full-on marketing strategies, performed by large firms with plans that are debated and designed around a conference table, can be quite effective yet at the same time can cost thousands to tens of thousands of dollars. But a grand-scale marketing scheme is not your only option, and you can actually be successful at marketing yourself with little to no financial investment. In this chapter, we'll only scratch the surface of marketing, but the intent is not to make you a good marketer of yourself as much as it is to help you recognize the value that a good marketing plan can bring.

In its simplest form, marketing is all about doing what you need to do in order to let others know about your value or your product. This process may come through word-of-mouth, or it may come from direct action on your part in the way of job applications, one-on-one discussions, or speaking engagements. The intent of each of these actions is to ultimately promote yourself to an audience that was not previously aware of what you have to offer. Therefore, having a successful self-marketing plan can serve to challenge the hand you were dealt by making others aware of your value(s). And because your challenge is typically designed with the intent of allowing you to pursue a better opportunity, arming yourself with your strongest attributes (i.e. your value) as well as reaching the right audience through successful planning and marketing will give you the best chance to be successful in your pursuits.

One of the first things you need to do is go back to that inventory you drew up of your skills, education, etc., which typically are the components of a good résumé. Even if you are simply wanting to start a new hobby, going through the process of outlining your strengths, level of training, interests, and education can help define who you are and where you will best fit in. By developing a framework of who you are, you can also determine where you will best fit in, whether that be from a value aspect or from an interest/passion/hobby aspect.

If you have mapped out your attributes such as your education, skills, etc., you now have the blueprint that will allow you to establish yourself. Spend time developing this blueprint, as it identifies your best qualities as well as those qualities that others can benefit from. What you write down is largely what others will be subjected to, so be sure to conduct a thorough self-evaluation of just who you are so that others will know as well. We'll look next at the example of the résumé as it relates well to how your best work attributes can be reflected in a single piece of paper, and it provides a good model for how it can help market yourself.

Résumé development is about as consistent as the day's weather. I have often told others that if you ask ten people how to draft a résumé, you will get 10 widely different responses. Therefore, don't expect to develop a 'perfect' résumé; rather, develop one that best highlights your personal and goal-related qualities. Remember, the résumé is designed to market your skills to a prospective hirer or supervisor, and a more detailed résumé better outlines the qualities you possess, which in turn defines your value should you be selected.

We won't get into the details of résumé development, as there are hundreds of books available focused specifically on that topic. Rather, we'll only discuss the use of the résumé for marketing yourself, particularly in how you must make clear your strongest qualities so that a potential employer sees the value that you can bring. Failure to do so results quite simply in your being passed over for the opportunity. Therefore, spend time thinking and organizing all of your qualities – whether work or personal, depending upon the ultimate use of your résumé – and develop them into a logical structure that allows a potential hirer to clearly see your value. Remember, the value you can provide is directly related to how much they are willing to pay you. Similarly, résumé s which do not convey a clear value will be overlooked, no matter the true quality of the applicant. If value cannot be gleaned from the résumé, it is effectively the same as indicating that there is no inherent value being offered.

Besides, the résumé, you must work to get your value as well as the quality of that value known among those who you plan to interact with. If, for example, you are trying to get into a specific school program to further your education, meet with the program director face-to-face if possible. An outstanding personality can help push through any potential flaws in an application. A similar situation should occur in the event you land a job interview – extoll your value; don't be shy yet at the same time you don't want to

126

come across as a braggart. Convince them in a brief conversation why you will be an asset to the program. The more you sell yourself to them, the more likely that you will advance through the process.

Don't think of marketing as some sort of financial commitment that you must make, such as often occurs through advertising or some other tool. Marketing can be done on a small-scale level with minimal investment as well, and doing so can often be just as effective for getting your value out to others. For example, you might be able to be a guest speaker at a small group, whether it be a book club or a local community club (e.g. Kiwanis or Lions club meeting). Outlining your story to them can help spread the word about what you can offer, and if you are an effective speaker you can also become known for your ability to capture an audience. Either way, you have to take the first step to get your name out there. To do so, think of small, inexpensive ways to help market yourself.

There are plenty of ways to perform cheap – if not free – advertising, many of which can help reach a wide audience. Writing a guest newspaper column or getting your story/situation on public access radio are relatively easy, particularly in that those types of media *need* to fill space, and you can provide the method by which to help fill the space they need. Volunteering your time at a relevant event – such as a car show if your desire is to become involved in car restoration – will allow you to mingle with other like-minded individuals, one of whom may be the initial contact you need to get your foot in the door. Writing a blog or posting on social media (e.g. Facebook,

Twitter), if done professionally, can help outline your intent as well as your qualifications in many cases. Much like resume development, there are many quality sources out there that can help you spread the word as to your personal value as well as your intent to become involved.

If you have the resources, you can certainly look to start advertising your services. If you have value such as motivational speaking that someone such as small business owners could benefit from, then advertising will certainly help you reach a wider market. You will have to find the medium (e.g. billboards, newspaper ads, etc.) that fits within a certain price point and still reaches an adequate number of people, but you will certainly be marketing yourself to a wide audience.

So why take the time to market yourself if you are wanting to improve the hand you were dealt? It's quite simple, really – it gives you the best chance to utilize others to help improve your opportunities. If you are wanting to enter a new profession, marketing can often get you similar results as can occur through strong networking. It helps others learn about you and possibly make the initial connection with you. Once that connection is made, it is up to you to sell that individual on your value. For example, if you send an email to a school inquiring about their business program, it might not seem like marketing, but you are letting the school know that you exist and that you have an interest in their program. Without your initial contact, you would not have made the connection with them, and they would have had no real way of knowing of your interest. Subsequently, they will contact you, in turn allowing you to convince them that you are the person that they need in their program. Similarly, you might be interested in learning how to play the piano. A simple email or social media post markets yourself enough to get a name referred to you. You can then tout your value (strong student, ample time to practice, etc.) that can help you find the best music teacher that matches your particular skills and assets. Once the connection has been made, you will have linked up with an individual that can help you improve your situation. To establish that initial connection, marketing can be a valuable tool in your quest to challenge the hand you were dealt.

Chapter 14 – Take caution on social media

Social media has become quite a catch-22 in our society. On the one hand it provides a convenient way to stay in touch as well as connect with others that we may have lost touch with. Yet, on the other hand, social media can be an outlet for many individuals to vent their frustrations and say things that they would not normally say without the relative anonymity that social media outlets can bring.

If you have had a few negative experiences in your life, you may have found that social media can be a lifesaver as much as it can turn into a detriment. For example, if you have been going through a divorce or have a particular medical condition, social media can allow you to join up with groups of other individuals in a similar situation where you all can discuss treatments, successes, etc. I myself belong to a few of these groups and have learned a few interesting and valuable bits of information here and there. In general, my experience on social media related to my own medical condition has been quite positive, and it would be my wish that your experience is equally favorable.

However, social media is far from roses and lollipops all the time. The ability for others to post what they want when they want, as well as the ability to add comments to almost any social media post can be problematic, especially for individuals (perhaps even you) who post personal issues online. It is not uncommon for someone to hide behind their online identity and start an argument, or make derogatory comments, or in some cases simply challenge the premise of your post. If this happens, the hope or intent you had for your post can be quickly diminished, and you are left with having to either delete your post, address the troublemaker, or attempt to ignore the situation altogether.

I once left social media for about 8 months. I can tell you that it was one of the most stress-relieving periods of time that I have experienced. I was actually driven to do so based not upon replies about myself or my situation, but rather about posts surrounding the 2016 presidential election. The anger, falsifications, misrepresentations, and outright vitriol that people whom I interacted with was downright scary. It got to the point that I would try to avoid reading many of the posts as they just seemed to form a knot in my stomach regardless of whether or not I agreed with them.

Eventually, the combination of my growing tired with the negative social media posts combined with my own lack of involvement led me to decide to just inactivate my account. At first I was a bit worried about missing out on relevant news as well as all of the funny posts and updates from friends. But I soon learned that there was a bigger benefit – I had more free time to play with my kids, interact to my wife, etc. I wasn't big on scanning social media during the normal day, but I did often check it in the evenings such as when they were watching a television show prior to bedtime. But, disabling my social media accounts effectively freed me up to do other things, and after a week or two of adjustment I quickly found that I had no desire to check social media.

A few months into my hiatus from social media, I had been hit up by far-away family members that they hadn't seen any updates of my kids. I realized quickly that my social media accounts were actually *their* connection to our family. It created a bit of a dilemma for me, as I needed to provide updates (e.g. photographs) of my kids so grandparents and friends could see what they were doing, but it would also mean getting back onto social media. So, I checked in with some friends to ask what the general tone was like online. By the third month, their reports indicated that it was somewhat safe to make my return to social media. I soon realized, however, that specific individuals were still at it, posting things that they were passionate about regardless of its validity. I also realized that most of these individuals were people who I may have known from years ago, but have no real interaction with other than social media. In effect, I had no reason to care about their interests or opinions. So, I did the 'unthinkable' – I removed them from my social media contacts.

Within days, I noticed that the tone on my social media pages cleared up dramatically. Even though I may have missed out on a few randomly important social media posts, the lack of general negativity was well worth any missed updates. To this day I have never had any negative effects or interactions with these individuals. Nothing along the lines of "why did you remove me" or anything like that. So for me, that gamble paid off. Granted, my own little experiment occurred around the time of an election, so I accept that there's quite a different climate around those events. Therefore, you may find that you have a much better or less negative online experience, and it is certainly hoped that this is the case.

Separately, I learned to avoid comment sections of online articles. If I read a story on a controversial topic, I would avoid scrolling to the bottom of the page where the generally anonymous comments would instantly start the vitriol again. My efforts weren't to attempt to live in some fantasyland of positivity. Rather, it was just to remove negative people and events from my life that I felt were preventing me from improving my situation. Even though I didn't have any direct effect of a particular news article, the high level of annoyance I found myself having with many of the online comments could be viewed as the equivalent of causing stress. And, I viewed stress as a detriment to my situation; therefore, removing sources of stress were beneficial to my situation.

Besides the potential for disagreements or arguments, remember too that social media allows the opportunity for you or your life to be seared permanently into history. If you make an unfortunate post or upload an image that you later regret, even if you take that post or picture down it is possible that someone has already recorded the image. As many of us know, a quick tap on a 'print screen' key can save a permanent record of your social media actions on some far-off computer. When you later decide that you want to make an improvement in your life, such as perhaps taking a leadership position, there's always the chance that your former post or picture makes an unwanted return at the most unfortunate of times. Therefore, think twice about anything that you post online, and ensure that you are comfortable even with any possible interpretation of what someone may think that you are implying. Online social media provides others a clear, concise, and factual representation of your actions, regardless of your own intent. Make sure that your contributions to social media are the kind that you won't later regret

Evaluate social media for your own situation. You certainly don't have to look at social media as a detriment; if you generally have great experiences online, use it to your advantage. But, given the relative anonymity that social media can offer, individuals can spew whatever they want with little repercussion. So, if you find that social media is detracting from your own progress, consider taking a hiatus or possibly removing those individuals responsible for any negative activity. It's your life and you are in control of it. If you feel that you have too much interaction with negative individuals, step up and eliminate the negativity which can include removing them from your social media links. As negativity gets removed from your life, the positives become much more pronounced. This increased positivity serves as an excellent challenge to the hand you were dealt, and most certainly will serve to improve your overall situation.

Chapter 15 – Set realistic goals

On the path to successfully challenging the hand you were dealt, it is easy to want to hurry through to the goal. For most of us, if we are in a bad situation we certainly want to improve our circumstances as quickly as possible. While this is certainly understandable, it is important that you work to keep a realistic timeline in mind when outlining your plan of attack as well as in setting your goals.

One of the big pitfalls many of us make when we take on a new challenge is that we overestimate the speed with which we will see results. We are excited, energized, and enthusiastic, and for some reason we think that our efforts will pay off in quick rewards. On working towards a goal to lose weight, we might expect to be 20 pounds lighter by the time our friend's wedding arrives in one month. Or we perhaps foresee being debt-free within a year. Sometimes, certain goals can be achieved despite a relatively short timeline; however, in most cases you can expect that making real change in challenging the hand you were dealt will take time.

Because you can expect a relatively drawn out timeframe for making real change, ensure that you set realistic goals. You have to adapt your behaviors and attitudes when it comes to making change, and the tactics that you use must be allowed to take shape over time. In some cases, word needs to get out about what you have to offer. In other cases, it takes time to learn a new skill. Or, you have to allow a process to occur slowly so as to set a strong foundation. For example, if you are marketing yourself as a speaker, don't expect to have a full schedule within a month of announcing your new business. You have to let the process gain momentum. Network, sell yourself to as many people as you can, and begin to make important connections. As we have discussed, you will never know which one of your connections is the one that gets you started, but by making as many connections as possible you help to ensure that word gets out about your abilities as a speaker. And once word does get out, expect to have to continue to work to keep your momentum going.

If you don't have a realistic timeline, you will ultimately fail at meeting your goal. It can be hard to recognize when our goals are unrealistic; therefore, be open to the constructive criticism we discussed earlier in this book. Allowing others to critique your goals can help you realize that your timeline is not realistic and as such you will not be on track to meet your goals. This allows you time to make adjustments to your schedule, thereby setting yourself up for success later.

Even if any failure was simply due to unrealistic goals, be aware that if you don't meet your goal you will invite the opportunity for negativity to creep in. If that occurs, be aware of subsequent self-doubt and a feeling of failure that often follows given that you did not meet your goal. Therefore, in order to help maintain a realistic path toward challenging the hand that you were dealt, ensure that you have been able to set a realistic goal.

It is important to understand that achieving a goal is largely a matter of willpower and whether you are able to make the changes necessary to accomplish your goal. Simply put, the more willpower you have, the more likely that you will meet your goal. The size of your goal may come into play as well, though. A small goal, like making it home in time to watch a football game on television isn't much of a major goal in the grand scheme of things. But buying a new home may be a lifelong goal of yours. Consequently, watching a game on television isn't likely to get any major effort out of you while trying to save for a new home often requires years of effort. Therefore, while both are goals, having a very small versus a very large goal can influence your motivation to reach that goal. And, they each require a unique type of effort. So while owning a home isn't by any means an unrealistic goal, it requires much more focus than what might be required for you to get home from work on time. However, if you are starting from scratch, owning a home cannot *realistically* occur in any short-term time frame. Therefore, because all of your goals have different factors involved, be sure to evaluate each of your goals individually rather than by one general method.

While we are on the topic of willpower and goals, let's also discuss the similar topic of the limits of your goals. Have you ever encountered an individual who had a major achievement, or met someone who was outstanding at what they do? It might be a rock star, or a professional athlete, or a fighter pilot. Or maybe you walked into an arena and marveled at what it must be like to be able to stand on stage and sing. So many of us are in a situation where we only dream of what it must be like to accomplish such a goal. Just the thought of *meeting* some famous individual or *being* in a famous place can give us enough excitement to last a year. But my question to you is this – why can't *you* be that person? What is stopping you from becoming famous, or easily recognized for your accomplishments? Truth be told, it's often that you have set limits on your own goals.

Setting limits on our goals also establishes our boundaries. We know from an earlier chapter that the 'lower' boundary is something that we are always trying to improve, always trying to raise the standard of. But what about the 'top' limit? What is the biggest goal we can achieve with enough time and resources? For some, that may be home ownership. For others, it might be meeting someone famous. But why can't you set a goal of *being* someone famous?

Think about that for a minute. In the same chapter that we are discussing not setting unrealistic goals I am telling you to set a goal such as becoming someone famous or someone whose accomplishments make them easily recognizable. In actuality, avoiding unrealistic goals and avoiding self-imposed limits on your goals are two very different topics. Unrealistic goals deal many times with timelines that aren't possible – losing 50 pounds in a month or being a millionaire by the time you are 30. Sure, each goal *could* happen. You could get liposuction or win the lottery. But because of the unlikeliness of either event actually occurring, you are stuck with reality. Can you lose 50 pounds? Sure! Can you do it in a month? No. Just like you most likely won't be a millionaire by age 30 with a traditional job. But, it doesn't mean that you can't set each as a goal. You just have to give yourself time and have the appropriate resources.

I remember standing in a library once when I was younger. Looking around at the books, I realized that *someone* had to be writing these books, and they must be absolutely amazing individuals. *Perhaps I could even do it*, I thought even back that a young age. At the time though, I didn't have the right training and I didn't have resources to write a book. And, I was just too lazy to try – so I didn't, for many years. Fast-forward about 30 years and now I have written several books. What happened? I had a realistic timeline and the resources. More specifically I had the training that allowed me to write more effectively, and I also had the online resources available that allowed me to publish a book. When set up correctly, this goal of mine – one of the many previously unreachable goals that I had set out for myself – was allowed to flourish. Once I quit glamourizing the mystique of book authorship and instead chose to become one myself, I realized that it wasn't some magical process that I had imagined it to be. Similarly, look at your own goals and map out just what it would take to accomplish them. Then, set an appropriate timeline that gives your goal(s) a real opportunity to happen.

Certainly for some of us, the time may have passed for a particular goal to become a reality. Perhaps you always wanted to become a fighter pilot but at 58 years old you're well past the legal entry age. While a fighter pilot may not have a possibility of happening, you certainly have other options. First, you could become a private pilot and end up experiencing the freedom of the open skies along with possessing many of the skills and attributes possessed by fighter pilots. Or you could book a flight in a jet aircraft using a professional service, perhaps even taking over the controls. While you may not have the opportunity to achieve *every* goal you establish, you can often find viable substitutes that are right in line with your original plans.

There's little doubt that many of us lack the patience to wait for something to occur the way we want it to occur. That is understandable; after all, we want to *win*. And we all certainly want to win when it comes to accomplishing our goals. In today's fast-paced society it can be hard to patiently wait for results when so much of what we need can be obtained almost immediately (think of the speed with which internet searches return you valuable information). When it comes to challenging the hand you were dealt, think of making positive change in your life as a marathon, not a sprint. As such, know that making those goals a reality will take time.

Many of the goals you will set are going to serve as strong challenges to your dealt hand, so each goal you accomplish will play a vital role in improving your overall situation. But remember that failure to set *realistic* goals can be detrimental to challenging your hand as you aren't giving yourself a chance to be successful. Therefore, set achievable goals. Study and accept the expected time it would take to get from your situation to the 'finish line' (i.e. accomplishing your goal) and plan out a timeline that allows the process to happen. And once you achieve your goal, *set another.*

Chapter 16: Focus on task completion

As we discussed in an earlier chapter, it can be human nature to be a bit of a procrastinator when it comes to getting a task done. If this is you, rest assured that you are like many, many others out there. I myself often find myself eagerly taking on a task or job, only to later realize that I have become bored and want to instead move on to something else, even if that original task remains unfinished. When we fail to take a task through to completion, we have to later go back and finish what we started, which can add further, unnecessary work to our schedule. Therefore, focus on developing a mindset that allows you to finish the assigned task at hand so that you have no lingering issues to deal with later.

A few chapters back, we discussed the notion of task management and how it can help to ensure that you utilize your time efficiently in order to accomplish your tasks in the most efficient manner possible. In a perfect world, all of your tasks will fit nicely into some sort of schedule that allows you to smoothly move from one task to the next. But, there are other times in which you don't have the luxury of fitting a task, chore, or major undertaking into a nice efficient 'slot' as it takes a significant amount of time to finish. The level at which a task becomes quite daunting is somewhat subjective, meaning that one person may look at a pile of dishes with such a level of disdain that they end up putting them off, while another person may feel that it takes something on a much grander scale, like painting their house, to cause them to avoid the task altogether. Regardless, the longer you put off task completion, the more it can be expected to eat at you until you finally take it on. But, once you have completed the daunting task, you will likely feel a sense of accomplishment, perhaps even to the point of feeling as though you should reward yourself.

If you are like me, taking on an intimidating task may require a figurative 'shove' to get you started. And, you may need several little shoves during the process itself in order to keep you on the road to completion. What I have found to help me comes from a technique known as 'fractionalizing'. Fractionalizing is based on the premise that you can be motivated through feeling as though you have accomplished at least *something*.

Using the fractionalizing technique, you divide the task up into sections, so that the summation of all sections equals 100%. So, if you're staring at a kitchen counter full of dirty dishes, break the area of your counter up into ten equal sections. If you clean the dishes in just one of those sections, you are $1/10^{th}$ of the way done. If you clean up two sections of dishes, you are $1/5^{th}$ of the way done. Double that amount of cleaned dishes, you are 2/5th of the way done. With just a few more dishes, you quickly realize that you are halfway done. If it only took you 15 minutes to get that far, simple math makes it clear that in 15 more minutes, you'll be done!

Personally, I fractionalize *everything*. The drive to work, the amount of time left in a meeting, mowing the yard, or any other somewhat long and/or tedious task I am currently engaged in. Even before I start on a task I have outlined the 1/4th point, the halfway point, and the 3/4th point so that I know at what point I have made significant progress. In establishing a definite endpoint, or the point at which the entire task is complete, I am able to mentally push through smaller sections of a task. This helps me see each minute of continued effort as a positive move toward the end-goal, and provides both motivation as well as a way of seeing progress.

Task completion is a vital part of challenging any hand you were dealt. The task could be as simple as cleaning a room or going from point A to point B. Or, the task could be as large in scale as getting a four-year degree. No matter the outcome, what is important is that you focus on getting the task done. In doing so you can limit future stress that can arise when you need to re-engage in a completed task. And, there is always a bit of satisfaction in getting a task done, particularly when you have done a good job. Therefore, work to avoid not only procrastination that arises in response to *starting* a task, but also ensure that you carry each task out to completion whenever possible. Though your reward upon completing your task may be that you have to start a new task, keep a positive outlook and recognize that one task has been accomplished in what may be a long list of pending duties. As you progress through your list of tasks, you will no doubt be improving your situation over time, which is the end-goal for ensuring task completion.

Conclusion

If you bought this book, there's a pretty good chance that are either going through some form of adversity or working your way back from some less-than-ideal circumstances. I sympathize with you. As I expressed across a few chapters, I have been there myself. And, I like you will almost certainly be there again at some point in the future. When I set out to write this book, my initial thoughts were to develop a text that would motivate an individual to not accept their current situation and instead fight to improve their situation and make it better. But as I thought about it more, I realized that I didn't want to write a motivational text. There are far too many books out there that spend a lot of effort in trying to build up the reader's confidence through telling them things like "you're a strong person" or "you can do this". While this type of effort has a purpose, I don't think that it's the best way for people to get things done. Rather, I feel that a roadmap of sorts, which can outline specifically what an individual needs to do to accomplish something in particular, is a much more effective way. That is what I intended to do with this book – to show you a pathway of many individual steps that you can use to improve your situation. And when you put all of these steps together, you can successfully challenge the hand you were dealt.

As discussed in the introduction of this book, we've all experienced adversity at some point in our life. Some of us are probably going through a bit of adversity even now. This issue is that with adversity, we *have* to deal with it because it absolutely impacts our lives. Much like when a baby is born, there's no avoiding the situation – you must address the situation no matter what else you have going on and no matter how much you want to avoid it. And much like parenting, adversity has no 'field guide' that outlines what we are supposed to do. Sure, there are a lot of books out there that deal with *specific* types of adversity, such as divorce, bankruptcy, or other major events, but it's almost guaranteed that they don't deal with our own precise set of adverse circumstances.

In knowing this, I wrote this book not to get you a way to solve your adverse event but rather to improve yourself beyond it. What you didn't find in this book was the legal process to deal with divorce, or how to fight a DUI offense, as each situation requires a very specific process that is well beyond the reach of this book. You have to own and accept those things, even if they weren't directly due to actions you took yourself (e.g. a spouse informed you that he/she is leaving you). In 'owning' your situation, it helps allow you to focus on the circumstances of your particular event, in turn allowing you to concentration on what you need to do to move forward. Remember, your situation is effectively the hand that life dealt you. This adverse event put you in a particular situation, and now you need to battle back to some level of normalcy. That is what this book was designed to do – to make you aware of ways to improve your situation: establish your value, find a passion. And then, market yourself, educate yourself, etc. Each small step we discussed in this book is one part of what you can do to give yourself the best opportunity to improve your situation. It may take a while, for sure. But in the end, you will look back on the journey to improve yourself and you will no doubt recognize the immense progress you have made. I wish you the best of luck in your journey, and I hope that you always continue to challenge the hand that you were dealt.

Other published books written by Mark Knoblauch

In addition to *Challenging the Hand You Were Dealt*, Mark has released five prior books, and is also working on several additional works. And, if you are interested in academic writing, be sure to watch for the release of his upcoming book detailing how to improve your professional writing skills.

Overcoming Ménière's. How changing your lifestyle can change your life.

ISBN# 978-1-7320674-7-9

Overcoming Ménière's provides the reader a detailed overview of Ménière's including the involved anatomy as well as the most recent research. By detailing his own Ménière's journey as well as what has worked for his own battle with Ménière's, Mark intends to provide other Ménière's sufferers a pathway which they themselves can following in order to find similar relief from the devastating effects of Ménière's disease.

Understanding BPPV. Outlining the causes and effects of Benign Paroxysmal Positional Vertigo

ISBN# 978-1-7320674-1-7

Benign Paroxysmal Positional Vertigo is a condition that triggers vertigo when the head is placed in a particular position. Furthermore, the vertigo ceases once the head is repositioned. Despite the somewhat forceful symptoms inherent to BPPV, the underlying cause of BPPV is relatively minor and can typically be fixed with a simple visit to a medical professional's office.

Because of his own experience with BPPV, Mark wrote *Understanding BPPV* so that everyone affected by this condition can have a solid resource guide outlining just what BPPV is, how it occurs, and how it is treated. Particular attention is focused on the anatomy of the ear, and how this anatomy is involved in generating the symptoms associated with BPPV. Mark also details the latest research into BPPV and provides an overview of the various diagnostic tests and treatments used to help BPPV patients in many cases get back to a vertigo-free life.

Essentials of Writing and Publishing your Self-Help Book

ISBN# 978-1-7320674-9-3

Some people elect to transform their own experiences and successes into a self-help book that outlines how they persevered through their difficult times. As a potential self-help book author yourself, you might be struggling to get started, get finished, or just need tips on how to finally get your advice and ideas onto bookstore shelves. *Essentials of Writing and Publishing Your Self-Help Book* is filled with information that will help walk you through the process of producing a quality self-help book. You'll be exposed to strategies that will help get you through the various stages of book production, gain insight into the options you have available for publication of your book, and review the individual steps and requirements necessary to get your advice from paper to a finished book.

Hidden down deep inside of us, we all have a book waiting to be written. The tips and techniques outlined in this book are designed to help you bring your ideas, successes, and lessons to life in the form of your own self-help book.

Outlining Tinnitus. A comprehensive guide to help you break free of the ringing in your ears.

ISBN: 978-1-7320674-2-4

The underlying cause of tinnitus has been described by researchers as one of the most controversial issues in medical science. Despite decades of intense research, the cure for tinnitus remains elusive. Consequently, millions of tinnitus sufferers are left susceptible to the frustration and annoyance brought about by the ever-present ringing in their ears. Mark Knoblauch has himself lived with tinnitus for over 15 years and understands the daily battles that occur in those individuals afflicted with tinnitus.

Now, despite still living with tinnitus daily, the high-pitched sound in his ear has become nothing more than an afterthought thanks to a dedicated treatment plan. And the success he had in addressing his own tinnitus drove him to write Outlining Tinnitus. This book is designed to serve as an all-inclusive guide for those individuals who suffer from tinnitus as well as those who live with or know someone suffering. Topics such as the involved anatomy, suspected causes, available therapies and treatments, and effects on quality of life are all discussed along with many others in order to provide a comprehensive overview of what tinnitus is as well as how it can be effectively eliminated.

The art of efficiency. A guide for improving task management in the home to help maximize your leisure time

(ebook)

In a world that seemingly never has enough time, we are often unable to get everything done that we need to accomplish in a given time frame. Though we can take out our frustrations on the fact that there is just not enough time in our day, no matter what we want, we can't simply create more time. Therefore, we have to make the most of the time we do have and try to utilize our available time in the most efficient way possible.

When it comes to getting tasks done in the home, efficiency can be the key to determining how much free time we ultimately earn for ourselves. As we become more efficient, we can expect an improvement in the amount of time available for us to use as we please. This book highlights those tactics that I have found beneficial at helping me get my required tasks done at home in the most efficient way possible. More importantly, this book will show you how to structure your tasks based upon the required activity level (i.e. active vs. passive tasks), in turn being able to schedule your time-on-task in a way that results in significant time savings due to your improved efficiency at task completion.

7 Ways to Make Running Not Suck

ISBN: 978-1-7320674-0-0

Let's face it – running sucks. Those pictures of runners that we see in advertisements showing a smiling, energetic runner in no way represent the agonizing, sweat-covered dread that so many of us put ourselves through in order to stay healthy. Given the vast amount of benefits associated with running, why can't it be more enjoyable?

What if you were told that running does not have to induce misery and can in fact be quite pleasant no matter your fitness level? You've read through the training books and learned how to adjust your nutrition, but what about the other issues that can affect your run? By accounting for several key factors involved with your run such as weather and equipment, you can minimize the opportunity for these same factors to have a negative impact on your run. This can in turn improve your running experience as well as your motivation to keep running.

Seven Ways outlines how to account for those ancillary factors that can directly influence the quality of your runs. Based on his own experience as well as the information gained from dozens of conversations with both new and experienced runners, Mark Knoblauch guides you through preparing and adapting to these factors as well as how to use them to your advantage.

By reducing the opportunity for negative influences to impact your running, it should be expected that your runs will become more enjoyable and more motivating, which in turn can have a significant impact on both your performance as well as your overall health.

Let others know!

If you found this or any of Mark's other books informative, *please take the time and post a review online!* Reviews help get exposure for the books and thereby improve the chances that others will be able to benefit from the material as well!

www.ingramcontent.com/pod-product-compliance
Lightning Source LLC
LaVergne TN
LVHW051410080426
835508LV00022B/3027